ELLO DUCK

The Life Journey of Mike Davis

MICHAEL DAVIS

Foreword

You might think that's a funny name for a book, *Ello Duck*. What's it all about? How to talk to our feathered friends in Duckese?

"'Ello duck" is a greeting used in the Midlands and Northern part of England that I grew up with when I lived in Lincolnshire. Some people drop their aitches, hence the spelling of 'hello'. Many people call you "duck" in the same way as the Australians call one another "mate". It is also used as an affectionate term sometimes with an added Y at the end. Like "'Ello, Michael ducky". If you are buying goods in a shop the assistant will most likely say the cost of the said item with "duck" at the end. "That will be £5.70, duck."

'Ello Duck is my affectionate way of greeting you and saying I would like to share my life's journey with you. I hope you enjoy this book as much as I have enjoyed writing it. I hope it somehow it helps and blesses you in your journey through this life.

The War

As I looked at the photo on the mantelpiece of the handsome, young man dressed in RAF uniform with his small hat tilted towards one side, I asked my mum, "Who is the man in this photo?"

"Ah," Mum said, "that's your Uncle Jim, your dad's brother. He was a rear gunner in a Lancaster in the war. He was killed in action. Your middle name is after Jim. You're not James, but Jim." I was only five or six years old when I asked Mum that question. The mantelpiece was in the front room which was special: it was kept spotless and we were only allowed in on a Sunday. I had often wondered who was in the picture. The war referred to, of course, was the Second World War.

It was 1954: rationing had only just stopped on the 4th of July. Living in Lincolnshire we were surrounded by RAF stations. The war years were fresh in the minds of my parents' generation and I heard countless stories of what it was like living in the war. Some stick in my mind forever, like the one where my dad was called out in the middle of the night to RAF Woodhall Spa. He was working in the maintenance department on the base. He was told to take off the wooden casing of a large crate. Within this crate was a barrel-like object. It was one of the prototype bouncing bombs designed by Barnes Wallis. My dad was sworn to secrecy, promising not to tell anyone what he seen. Guy Gibson, who was head of the famous Dam Busters, frequented the local pub called the Blue Bell Inn. He also used the Petwood Hotel in Woodhall Spa, and they have not changed that room where the officers met since the war ended.

I had adopted aunts and uncles at that time, meaning real close friends of the family. One of these uncles was Uncle Frank who ran a greengrocer's shop from one of our buildings near our house. Uncle Frank told me stories of the war and what it was like driving in blackout conditions. One night he ran into the main junction box on an RAF base. It took out all the lights in the base. Many expletives were used back and forth venting frustration and anger!

The house I grew up in was a three-bedroomed semi-detached house. It was unusual as it was split in two, long ways on. The property had outbuildings across from the house, leaving a middle yard driveway. The outbuildings consisted of a coalhouse with a pigsty at the end, then another room where Dad kept his car, leading to a workshop, and finally another room facing the main road that Uncle Frank used as his greengrocer's shop. Our garden was enormous with five or six apple trees, a plum tree and finally, at the far end, a larger chicken run. In the war years the fruit trees, chicken run, pigsty and garden helped feed the family. I had a sister fourteen years older than me, Janet, and a brother called Keith who was ten years older. So I was doted on, being the baby of the family. They both remember the war years, too, telling of how hard those times had been.

My dad was a clever man who never reached his full potential. He was sent to live with his aunt who had awful health problems. Dad worked on the land, forgoing any further education as he had to earn money to pay for drugs to keep his aunty alive. He wanted to be a civil engineer. After aunty died he did correspondence courses in electrical engineering. He taught himself plumbing and had his own business as a plumber. I was told that, when I was just three years old, I knew all the tools used in plumbing. Apparently if Dad was down a hole in the ground mending a pipe leak he could ask for any particular tool and I would pass it down to him. He had a good business but, alas, it was not to last. When I was about six years old I watched him going with a small suitcase out of the yard. He was picked up by a friend who took him to Leicester General Hospital. He had lung cancer. I learnt much later that the surgeon had had to cut away a third of one of his lungs which had the tumours in.

After this major operation Dad wasn't able to carry on with the plumbing business as it was too physical.

After a while he obtained a job in the Air Ministry of Public Building and Works at RAF Hospital Nocton Hall. He was a supervisor doing administrative work mainly. It was a poorly paid job which meant us living a frugal lifestyle. I remember feeling ashamed of us having lino in the hallway with holes in it because we couldn't afford to have any new lino. Fitted carpets were a big luxury we couldn't afford. Mum used to work part-time cleaning people's houses and cleaning in the pub across the road. She could make a meal out of next to nothing. Mum used the eggs from the chickens and the apples plus any produce we grew in the garden. Once a week the egg man called to collect the eggs, which also helped the family budget.

Today we often say we have to do the washing, which means putting the clothes in a machine with some washing powder and pressing a button. In those days my mum would get up at six am on a Monday morning, fill with water the copper boiler, and light the fire below it which was housed across in the outbuildings. Then boil the white sheets in the copper: she would use a tub with water and soap in it, called a dolly tub, to wash clothes using a dolly, which was a three-pronged wooden affair with a handle at the top to agitate the clothes in the tub. After washing in this manner, all the clothes had to be rinsed in cold, clean water that was pumped up from a well below the outbuildings. Once rinsed the clothes then had to go through a contraption called a mangle. The mangle rollers squeezed the water out of the clothes which were then ready to hang on the washing line. After the clothes were dry they had to be ironed using flat irons that were warmed at the fireplace. The whole process took all day Monday to complete as long as the weather was fine. Today we have it so easy.

My grandad, Frank Davis, was quite a village character. He used to be a butler in service when he was working. Anytime we visited Grandad and Grandma for a cup of tea, the silver tray would come out with the silver teapot along with the best bone china. He made you feel like royalty and special: we all had to be on our best behaviour when visiting my grandparents. Grandad used to come round to our garden to take care of the beehives and prune our roses. Grandma was a regal-looking woman with her bleached white hair who had raised and looked after her six children in some difficult times. It was the fashion in my grandparents' day to have stuffed animals to show off in the homes in glass cases, anything from squirrels, foxes, owls, or large fish like chub. I found them both fascinating to visit and liked listening to their stories of what it was like working in service for the wealthy.

We didn't have a TV until I was about twelve years old. Eventually we rented a black and white TV set from Rent-a-vision for so much a week. We used to have a guy with a projector and screen who used to set himself up in the village hall to show films like

Superman, Old Mother Grady or a Norman Wisdom film. When I was very young I grew up listening to the radio: radio was my friend with all its funny noises as it was turned on or tuned to another programme. Radio stars had come through from the war years like Vera Lynn, the forces' sweetheart, George Formby with his cheeky grin and happy songs. Gracie Fields, the Lass from Lancashire with an amazing voice, and The Crazy Gang, with Bud Flanagan and Ches Allen. All these artistes kept the morale of the forces high in the war years which overflowed into the difficult years after the war. There were such programmes as Workers' Playtime, where the outside broadcasting unit would visit factories to make a lunchtime show to encourage workers in the war. We huddled around the radio listening to programmes that took us to another world: Journey into Space; Dick Barton the detective; and comedy shows such as Round the Horne with Kenneth Horne, Sidney James and Kenneth Williams. There was The Clitheroe Kid, not a western but stories of a mischievous boy getting into all sorts of scrapes. Not forgetting Archie Andrews, a ventriloquist dummy on radio. It sounds crazy, but we used to listen to his calamities each week. Then of course there were The Goons with Spike Milligan, Harry Secombe, Peter Sellers and Michael Bentine: this comedy was ahead of its time. I still like listening to The Goons' recordings. Sometimes my parents used to go to live shows put on by these radio stars. One year when I was still very young we went all the way to London to go to the Palladium Theatre to see The Crazy Gang, Tiller Girls, Max Bygraves and others go through their routines and acts. I still remember Bud Flanagan and Ches Allen singing "Strolling", and Max Bygraves standing in a white mac telling gags.

The radio was the medium by which Winston Churchill had solemnly announced to the nation of Great Britain with great gravity, "We are at war with Germany." All the plans for a rosy future were suddenly destroyed. The British, being British, made the best of what they had and came out fighting hard, rising to the challenge. It was this post-war culture I was born into in July 1949 with all the memories of war still fresh in people's minds.

Grow Up

"Why don't you grow up, boy?" my sister yelled. I was always fooling around and getting on people's nerves. I think I was what you call a hyperactive child. When I was young I was given a small, white tablet: I think this was to calm me down. In our family, one never spoke in plain English about any infirmities, diseases or operations. If someone had an operation, the conversations about it were always in a hushed tone, along with a strange pulled face. "She's had them out," was sometimes the phrase. What had been removed was down to guesswork on my part, at any rate. Daily, I had to take these little, white tablets: if they were supposed to calm me down, they didn't work! I was on the go all the time, except if I wanted to build something with Meccano or make something with Plasticine. Then I would silently build myself a crane, tractor or dinosaur. I was very disruptive in infant and junior school, always playing the fool. Later on in life they discovered I needed glasses. Maybe that's why I didn't concentrate on what was being taught because I couldn't see the blackboard clearly. That's my excuse anyway.

Next door to where we lived was the village blacksmith. I used to love going round there and pumping the bellows for the fire. Sometimes I made a poker on the anvil. I loved seeing the horses being shod and the blacksmith making things. I had good friends at this time and we often went fishing in the local River Bain. We caught perch, gudgeon, roach, bream and sometimes chub. I loved fishing in this local river it was really good fun. We went to friends' farms and played cowboys and Indians or pretended to be fighting in the war. On Saturday mornings Mr Harvey brought a few horses to the local playing field. We paid our two and sixpence for a ride on his horses.

On a Sunday I was made to go to Sunday school at Coningsby Baptist Church, not for any deep spiritual reason, but because the Sunday school was put on in the afternoon, it meant Mum and Dad could have a bit of peace and quiet. The main teacher was Mrs Franklin, helped by her close friend. They often used to roll their eyes up or have a face of shock horror when I was being disruptive. I still remember the songs we sang with words like "Twelve men went to spy out Canaan, ten were bad, two were good", "I am HAPPY", and "Zacchaeus was a very little man". I didn't really appreciate or understand the true meaning of all these songs. It was just a fun time on a Sunday afternoon.

Once a year we had the Harvest festival which

was a big event for the Baptist church. The farmers brought in sheaves of corn, big bags of potatoes, cauliflowers, leeks, carrots and cabbages. The Sunday school class was given recitations to memorise ready to speak out on the big day. The service was usually held in the afternoon. The place was packed out. The Sunday school children had to sit on benches that had been placed on a temporary stage in the church. We all had our best clothes on with shoes highly polished, hair brushed, faces cleaned. My dad said, "When it's your turn to give your recitation, make sure you lift your chin up, open your mouth wide and speak out loud and clear," which I duly did, without hesitation. Even now if I'm speaking in public, I speak out loud and clear. The church resounded to the congregation singing at the top of their voices, songs like "Tell Me the Old, Old Story".

Prize-giving was another event at the church I loved. The prizes were usually storybooks about Jesus, Joseph or Moses. One year I did get the book *Treasure Island* by Robert Louis Stevenson. I think I've still got it on my bookshelf. Towards Christmas we had the Christmas Party with games and lots of nice food.

When I was twelve it was mainly girls who attended, plus one lad who was a bit of a geek. At the time this didn't fit my new interest and image of becoming a mod, I was more interested in The Beatles, The Rolling Stones and the Merseybeat sound.

My parents were God-honouring but not attending any church, much like most people just after the war. My mum was very superstitious. If we broke a mirror, it was seven years' bad luck; never cross on the stairs; never walk under a ladder; and so on. When I was about five or six years old I had warts all over my hands. Mum had put various chemicals on the warts to burn them away but they still remained. My hands were covered in warts with black stuff on them. One day I was taken by my mum on a long walk to see a man who was a "charmer". He held my hands for a few minutes and then told my mum the warts would be gone in the morning. My mum paid the man for his service and we left for the long walk home.

I was awoken by Mum the next morning only to find my hands completely clear of any warts. I found out much later the source of the charmer's power. Mum never turned gypsies away and mostly bought something off them, or offered a glass of water. Sometimes she had her fortune told her by these gypsies. When visiting Skegness seaside town, just for a laugh Mum and Aunty Flow would go in to see a Rosie Lee character and have their fortunes told. Strangely enough, I was always singled out in our family as being special by these tellers. To add to all this darkness, I used to hear my dad tell stories of horses not going down a certain lane or road because a witch had cursed it. Then there were the water dowsers finding the best pace to drill a well.

Our house, I was told, was haunted by a soldier returning from WW1. My bedroom was at the end of a passageway. At the end of the passageway was my parents' bedroom door. As I lay in bed one night I saw a white figure entering my mum and dad's bedroom. I thought it was Jesus, so I called out "Jesus" and the figure duly disappeared. Later on in life I was to find out why this figure went as I had spoken the name Jesus.

After failing the Eleven Plus, I attended Gartree Secondary Modern School in the adjoining village of Tattershall. Tattershall is the next village to Coningsby, famous for having one of the only brick medieval castles in the country, built by Ralph, 3rd Baron Cromwell, in the 15th century. I grew up in the village of Coningsby in Lincolnshire, which had one of the largest RAF stations in the country. Consequently there were a lot of RAF children attending the schools. The spin-off was that civilian children were allowed to go to the cinema and social club on the camp. At that time the Vulcan bomber was stationed at Coningsby. As a result, if a Vulcan was going overhead it made such a loud noise one had to stop conversing until the plane passed. At weekends the planes didn't fly so it gave us all a break from the loud noise.

On my thirteenth birthday my Aunty Vera turned up with a large present and put it down in front of me on the dining room floor. As I opened the present Aunty's eyes lit up with delight as she watched my face. Wow, it was a Dansette record player! I could now play the latest records by The Beatles, Rolling Stones etc. The player had pride of place in the front room. I was allowed to go to the front room to play my records over and over again at full volume. I just loved my present from Aunty Vera, who was South African. She had married my dad's brother Bader. They had children and when they all grew up they moved to Leeds. I haven't seen them since.

I was still a bit of a pain regarding education. I liked playing the fool and found most subjects too hard or boring. We used to get one teacher in particular who was easily distracted into talking about the war instead of rural science, and we just knew what to say to lead him off-track. I did like history, art, geography and woodwork, though. My favourite subject was science. I had a great science book at home which I devoured. I wanted to be an inventor and design a man-powered plane. I had a go at making a radio from a kit I bought from a magazine called *Practical Wireless*. The trouble was that I was trying to solder using one of my dad's soldering irons used in plumbing. This meant heating the iron in the fire before doing any soldering. I really should have had an electric soldering iron. Needless to say the radio didn't work too well due to what they call dry joints. I managed to get BBC Radio 3. The "in" station at that time was Radio Luxembourg, so Radio 3 wasn't what I was hoping for.

I just wasn't interested in school. There were much more exciting things happening in the world of pop music, a revolution. A number of us went to Lincoln Odeon to see the latest bands. In one night we saw The Kinks, Rolling Stones, Dave Clark Five, The Searchers, Cilla Black, Gene Pitney, The Mojos and others. It was all very exciting. I didn't do very well at all at school, except in science.

I went to Gartree School at the age of eleven years old, not knowing anything about sex or the opposite sex. When I was younger, I had had two very good friends who were girls. One was a bit of a tomboy, so liked climbing trees and kicking a ball about. It never crossed my mind that girls were different. One day in the playground at Gartree a lad, a few years older, was going on about a particular girl he fancied to a few of us younger lads. He was saying he would love to have sex with this particular girl. I innocently said, "What do you mean?" He then explained the facts of life. No one had ever explained all this to me. There was no sex education at school at that time. That's how I was given sex education at the age of just over eleven years. A few years later, as testosterone kicked in, I, too, wanted to have sex with girls I fancied but never got anywhere near my desire. Miniskirts were the fashion which drove us young teenager lads crazy. Girls at school were told to lower their skirts to knee level and keep their blouses buttoned up. This helped us to concentrate a bit on what was being taught. We all had desires on certain female teachers, too, who we fancied. I seem to remember the history teacher was very sexy. All the lads raced to the History lessons, not to learn history but just to see the teacher.

I was useless at getting off with any girls whatsoever. All I could do was fantasise. I didn't have a real girlfriend until I was just over eighteen. I was very skinny, gangly-looking lad with a spotty face and I wore National Health glasses. I felt I was ugly. I was so thin I could see my heart beating in my ribcage. I hated getting changed for PE lessons in case any of the other boys took the Mickey out me. I was ashamed of my body. I was so thin mainly because of my diet. Mum used to cook really lovely roast dinners or casseroles, but I wouldn't eat such meals, to my dad's annoyance. Often mum would go the kitchen and make up a bowl of porridge for me instead. I had porridge morning, noon and night. Consequently, I had no stamina for sports at school, I was a weakling. As well as this, I had a low self-esteem and felt inferior to everyone else. I hid this by fooling around and making people laugh. Mum was really worried about me being so thin and took me to the doctor for a check-up to see why I had an aversion to meat and vegetables, and why I was so thin. The doctor assured my mum there was nothing wrong with me and my body was functioning perfectly normally. He said that I had a strong, big bone structure and I would fill out as I got older. This proved to be the case, and eventually I filled out and got stronger. My sister at last saw me growing up as the years went on into teenage life. I left school when I was fifteen years old without any qualifications to my name. What should I do next?

Work

Every Friday night was Youth Club night held in the village hall in Tattershall. Nothing fancy, just a Dansette record player, small billiard table, table tennis table along with snacks and soft drinks. All us teenagers met up for a bit of fun and showed our superegos off to one another. One Friday night an older guy called John Goose asked what job I was doing since leaving school. "Nothing," I replied. John said, "Why don't you come and work for me and Dad at the butcher's shop?" "Ok," I replied.

That's how I started my career in the meat trade, having left school at fifteen years old. I could have gone for some sort of work on the RAF station in Coningsby. I knew if I did that I would be there for life. My father advised us children to get a trade: you can deviate away from it, but at least you will always have something to fall back on if things didn't work out. He believed that was a Jewish tradition that worked for them. My sister trained as a hairdresser in Boston; my brother trained as a carpenter in Woodhall Spa.

So I started working as a butcher boy at J R Goose & Son for £3.00 a week. Start at 8am, finish at 6pm, with one hour lunch break Monday to Saturday with half-day Wednesday. Monday was sausage making and scrubbing out fridges. Nearly every butcher's shop had their own slaughterhouse out the back in those days. Monday afternoon the animals were delivered to the premises to be put into the pen ready for slaughter. Usually Mr Goose went to Sleaford Market in the morning and bought a couple of heifers and five or ten sheep. We started slaughtering at about 3pm and finished around 8 or 9pm. After each animal was killed and eviscerated. It was my job to empty the paunch's contents into a wheelbarrow and take to the bottom of the garden for manure. I had to then wash the paunches out in cold water ready for collection next day. I had a continual dolly tub of cold water running so that I could get bucket after bucket of water to throw down and scrub the outer concrete causeways surrounding the buildings. After the butchers had slaughtered it was my job to clean pens out and scrub walls with cold water. We all then scrubbed and cleaned the slaughterhouse. Mondays were the hardest and longest day of the week. The rest of the week consisted of taking customers' orders out using the errand bike, the kind with a big basket at the front, making sausages, scrubbing and cleaning premises, going out with John or Mr Goose in the butcher's van on a round selling meat. Something rather strange happened. I suddenly acquired a large appetite for meat. People told me it was because I was working every day amongst the meat that gave me this newfound appetite. Instead of a bowl of porridge I would now have, for example, two pork chops with a large amount of vegetables, followed by a large portion of apple pie or egg custard and a pint of milk. After a year of this kind of diet I began to get growing pains all across my chest. I grew bigger and stronger by the day.

One Monday night I had the following experience. The first heifer had been killed and was being dressed by John and another butcher. The second heifer was still in the pen waiting to be slaughtered. There was a gun on the table just outside the slaughterhouse door. This gun was called a captive bolt or humane killer. A cartridge was inserted into the gun and then held against the animal's head. When the trigger was pulled a bolt six inches long inside the gun was fired into the animal's head which stunned it. The animal then had its main artery cut and this completed the kill. It's a very humane way of slaughter, as all the animal feels is something held against its head. Sometimes after the gun had been fired the cartridge would get stuck in the gun. To get it released you cocked the gun mechanism back and fired it: this made the dud cartridge spring out when opening the gun up. This particular night I saw the gun on the table with a cartridge in. I thought it was a dud cartridge so was going to fire it like normal to get the cartridge out. Unbeknown to me, John had put a live cartridge into the gun ready for the next heifer. Me, being me, fooling about, put the gun to my head and pulled the trigger. As I pulled the trigger a hand grabbed my wrist and moved it about an inch. The gun went off: the captive bolt went past the top of my head by a millimetre. The butchers stopped work and came outside. Mrs Goose came out of the house to see what was going on, she knew the time for the second heifer to be stunned was too soon after the first one. I just stood there in shock. The hand that moved my wrist I now believe was the hand of an angel, as no one was near me when I fired the gun off. If the captive bolt had gone into my head it would certainly have killed me. God had His hand on my life, even though I didn't know Him. It's certainly by God's grace and mercy that I am here today.

After about a year I was given the responsibility of stunning and sticking the sheep with a knife in the throat to get them ready for the butcher to finish dressing. Every Tuesday morning the Meat Inspector came to inspect the carcases to make sure they were all fit for human consumption. He was always in a very clean, white, well-pressed coat. I used to think then that that's the sort of job I would like to do. I carried on in this job learning the trade for just over two years.

Saturday nights after finishing work at 6pm I used

to rush home, get washed and changed ready to go out. I and a few friends used to bike four miles to the dance at Woodhall Spa in the Jubilee Hall. Usually there was a live band playing the latest songs from *Top of the Pops* TV programme. The girls used to put their handbags down on the floor and make a circle and dance round them. I just used to watch the band and stand at the side of the hall. Because I had an inferiority complex I wouldn't dare ask a girl for a dance. I was afraid of being rejected. We all enjoyed the live music at full volume and we fooled around a bit. Sometimes there was fights at the dance especially if the rockers turned up on their motorbikes. It was the mods and rockers era and my friends and I leant towards being mods except we didn't have the scooters, just pushbikes!

The other place we went to was the Castle Club on the RAF station. They had some up and coming bands play like The Hollies and The Tremeloes. The usual thing of the girls dancing round handbags and us standing on the edge of the room carried on. The older lads got the girls. During the week we hung out at one another's houses or the local café in Tattershall.

I don't remember ever going away on a family holiday with my mum and dad when I was growing up. I think it's because we were too poor. When I was seventeen I set off on the road, thumbing lifts to the Lake District. I travelled all around the Lakes, staying in youth hostels. At one of the hostels I met a French guy called Gerrard and we went round the lakes together as friends looking at all the sites. Gerrard was studying to be an oceanographer at a university in Marseilles in France. A few years later I went to stay with him in Marseilles for a holiday. I remember the old port with cafés on the side and people sitting having coffee and watching the world go by.

One night when I got home from work my mum and dad sat me down and said they had something important to tell me. They had decided to move to live in Lincoln. They were big fans of a TV programme called *Coronation Street*. I think they felt they would be happier living in a terraced house like depicted in the TV programme in Lincoln where one of their friends had moved to live.

I left J R Goose in Tattershall when I was just over seventeen years old to move to Lincoln. I obtained a job as a butcher's apprentice in the Co-operative Society. The shop I worked in was down Monks Road which was about half an hour's bike ride from Manby Street, where we lived. The butcher manager at the Monks Road shop had a false leg. He had lost his leg in an explosion in the war. I was delivering customers' orders on my butcher's bike up and down the steep roads either side of Monks Road. It was hard work but no slaughtering as the meat was delivered twice a week. The usual scrubbing and cleaning was all part of the job. I liked fooling around at this time. I had bought a joke rubber thumb which had been painted red to look just like blood. One day I was at the butcher's block in the shop with the joke thumb. I brought down the cleaver really hard onto the block, screamed, then threw the thumb into the middle of the shop. One of the customers screamed and fainted, thinking I had cut off my thumb.

I had no friends to go out with at this time, so I got a bit low and lonely. Then I saw an advert for a folk club at the Turks Head in Lincoln. I went to the said folk club gingerly poking my head into the upper room over the pub. I was welcomed in with open arms. John and Maureen Pape ran the folk club and took me under their wing. At that time the folk scene was big in Britain. We had up and coming stars such as Maddy Prior and Tim Hart, Peggy Seeger. Maddy and Tim shocked the folk world by going electric when they formed Steeleye Span. One visitor really impressed me greatly called Stefan Grossman. Stefan is a country-blues guitarist from New York. The sounds he got out of his guitar were amazing, it was the first time I had heard bottleneck blues. After hearing him play I bought my first guitar from a second-hand shop in Lincoln. I still remember my first guitar, it was an Eko steel-strung. My guitar became my friend: I sat for hours in my bedroom learning how to play the guitar. (I'm still learning!) I got fully into the folk scene, visiting other clubs and making new friends. Along with the music was the drinking and some drugs. I kept away from drugs at this time but liked to drink a bit. I did still to go to a few dances but really felt out of place. I loved the folk singers and musicians. My social life was sorted, I had great times with my new friends in the folk scene. I also went to evening classes to study art, where I made friends in the art scene. I used to go to some of their way-out parties. One night I did try smoking cannabis and collapsed on the floor.

In the next street to where we lived there was a man called George and his wife. George was blinded by shrapnel in the war: he had been given a crystal ball whilst in the war overseas by a local man. George used to have people round to look into the small crystal ball and tell them what they saw. He would then interpret the pictures. Mum and Dad and friends used to go round to see George quite a lot to have their fortunes told in this way. I went a few times and saw all sorts of pictures which George then interpreted for my future. We also used to have a gypsy come round to our house called Maud. Maud used to do fortune-telling, too, using tea leaves or eggs in a glass. I was curious about spiritual things and once or twice I visited a spiritualist church in Lincoln. I wondered how the medium contacted the dead and how what she said about the deceased was so accurate. Of course the deceased always assured the family that he or she was fine and really enjoying life on the other side. I was also convinced that there must be life on another planet out there. I believed in UFOs and all the stories of aliens abducting people. I was always curious, though, why the abductees never brought anything back with them to prove they had been on a spaceship. Surely they could have taken something while the alien was looking the other way? Later, I was to discover the truth about all the above.

I attended night school once a week in the local technical college. One night one of the lads was saying that J Sainsbury was visiting the city to recruit staff. They were setting up a mobile recruitment wagon in the middle of Lincoln. J Sainsbury at that time was a southern company and they recruited people from the north. I went along for an interview and a week later I had a letter offering me a job in the Crawley store. I was only eighteen so my mum and dad were worried I would be alright. On my side I was just really excited about going on an adventure: little did I know what was going to happen next.

New Life

As I walked out of the railway station at Crawley, suitcase in hand, I had a spring in my step. I was so excited about starting a new job in a new place I had never been to before. It was January 1968: Crawley was a New Town which had modern buildings with an overspill of people from London. Everything looked so fresh and new. I found Queens Square where Sainsbury's store was located. I introduced myself and I was taken upstairs to meet the housekeeper Mrs Johnson, who showed me to my room on the third floor overlooking Queens Square. At that time Sainsbury's had live-in staff above their shops. Every shop had a housekeeper to cook for the store's staff as well as the live-in staff. All my meals were cooked for me and a washing machine was in a utility room near my bedroom. For my first time away from home it was luxury. After a cooked breakfast at 7am I just walked downstairs to work in the shop. There were three other lads living upstairs with me all in our separate bedrooms: Ray, Tollo and Paddy. It was fun to be together. At that time there were about ten butchers in the Crawley store. The meat arrived as full carcases which we then cut and prepared for the ladies to wrap and pack. The ladies sat either side of an open rectangle refrigerated unit; we placed the different cuts of meat into metal trays into this unit. The ladies had all the different size of trays and film to wrap the meat ready for display. Compared to now, the whole system was very labour-intensive.

As I settled into the job and way of life I was still full of energy and liked fooling around to make people laugh. The store was a semi-self-service-type meaning we still had a meat counter at the back of the shop, as well as packaged meat in the refrigerated display units. We took it in turns manning the counter serving the public with specific joints of meat or liver which wasn't easy to pre-pack. One day it was my turn to be on the counter. For a laugh I removed some pig's eyes from a carcase and placed one on my forehead, parting my hair either side of the eye. Then went on to the counter at the back of the store. A lady customer came along and was pointing to a joint of beef that she wanted. I closed my eyes and bent forward asking her to point to the joint. She then looked at me seeing the eye looking at her: she let out a frightening scream and nearly fainted. I was reprimanded by the manager for scaring the customers. One day we had some New Zealand lamb delivered to the store packed in dry ice instead of frozen. There was a trial going on with New Zealand lamb packed in this way. I put some of the dry ice into a bucket of water which then made a vapour-like steam. I took the bucket out to the counter. Soon there was vapour billowing out all around the counter and into the shop. The customers thought there was a fault with the refrigerated counter. We just said, "Everything is ok, madam: an engineer is on his way." There was a lot of fooling around out the back of the store the customers knew nothing about.

There wasn't much entertainment in Crawley at this time. There was the local cinema they called the fleapit and the Starlight Ballroom, plus a bowling alley. Of course there were the pubs scattered around the town. I got involved with a few people playing guitar and wanting to form a rock band. We played in one of their houses: mainly we didn't get any gigs. It was just fun to play with a group of musicians. One or two of the group were into drugs which thankfully I didn't get into. Tollo and I did go to a folk club once in Soho, London, called Les Cousins. We went to the 11pm till 6am slot and saw Stefan Grossman. Someone in Sainsbury's organised a night out to Empire Pool Wembley to a show put on by *Melody Maker* or *New Musical Express*. We saw The Rolling Stones, Walker Brothers, Gene Pitney, Status Quo, Dave Dee, Dozy, Beaky, Mick and Tich and others all in one show. It was a great night out. Sometimes we used to all go to the Orchid Ballroom near Purley to dance the night away to live music.

We had an au pair girl come to help the housekeeper in Sainsbury's called Aila Pulkinin who was from Finland. Aila became my first proper girlfriend. We went out to pictures or dances together and we visited London where I showed her the sites. At Christmas time because she had no family in the UK, I took her home to have Christmas with the Davis family. I took Aila to the folk club in Lincoln and introduced her to John and Maureen. Aila was a lovely girl. I really liked her we had some laughs together. She mixed well with all my friends. Alas, time came for Aila to go back to Finland and that was the end of our relationship. I used to write to her in Finland now and again I kept in touch.

One of the butchers called Charles was different to the rest of us: he always had a smile on his face, he was a cheerful guy. Charles used to wear small badges with "Jesus Saves" or "Jesus Lives" written on them. Every now and again he would invite Tollo and me to a Christian meeting in Crawley or London. I felt uncomfortable in these big meetings. Almost every time the speaker would invite people to come to the front for some reason. I just didn't understand what these meetings were all about. Charles used to give out gospel tracts for us to read. (Gospel tract was a small leaflet with a short story giving a gospel message.) Invariably these tracts ended up in the dustbin unread. I did keep one or two but never got round to reading them. One night, though, I returned to my room above Sainsbury's store quite drunk. I had met up with friends and we went round a few pubs drinking heavily. I flopped down on my bed and I saw one of Charles's gospel tracts. In this tract there was the story of a man called Bill on his way home from a night out in the pubs. All of a sudden a car came round the corner at speed, it skidded on some oil in the road. The car mounted the pavement and went straight into Bill and killed him instantly. Then the story said that Bill went straight to Hell because he never received Christ into his life. At this point I instantly became sober. Hell, I thought, surely there isn't a place called Hell. Heaven, yes, I believed there was a place called Heaven from my Sunday schooldays. I thought if there is a place called Hell I don't want to go there. I thought I must settle this question once and for all time while I am young, so that I can carry on drinking and chasing girls, enjoying myself. I am going to prove that there isn't a Hell and no God to stop me having a good time.

A few nights later some friends from the shop came round to see us in the flats. They wanted to have a séance. What's a séance I said? Well, it's where we contact the dead and ask questions. We set these lexicon cards out in a circle on the table to form the alphabet and put an upturned glass in the middle of it. Then we all lightly touch the glass and the glass moves to different lexicon letters on the table to answer our questions. It is a real fun thing to do, they said. We proceeded to set it all up and we all put our finger lightly on the glass. We asked to meet certain dead people like Lord Nelson or King Henry VIII, asking questions, and the glass moving to the letters to spell out the answers. Then after about half an hour of this I asked to meet Jesus. At this point the glass rushed around the table and off into the wall. One of the friends went running down the corridor screaming and the whole session ended.

I was left wondering what that was all about. The next day, I told Charles what had happened in our apartment above the shop. For the first time ever Charles face went really serious and troubled. He said you weren't contacting the dead, you were contacting evil spirits called demons imitating the dead. What? I thought Demons? Some time after I was thinking if there are demons and a Devil and His Kingdom there must be angels, Jesus and His Kingdom. I thought I must prove this to be wrong and just trickery of the mind. I talked to Charles some more in our tea breaks at work. He invited me to come round to his house and have a chat with him and his wife Eileen. "Alright, then, I'll come tomorrow night at eight o'clock." Right, I thought, I'll get all my arguments ready to prove that all this about Jesus and the Devil is a load of rubbish.

Charles and Eileen lived in Langley Green in a small council house with their two small children. I duly arrived at 8pm on Thursday, the 8th of May, ready to thrash out the topic all guns blazing. Charles said before we start talking, I want to read this story from the Gospels. Oh, ok, I thought. Charles read out the Bible from John chapter three. It was all about a man called Nicodemus, a ruler of the Jews, who came to see Jesus at night to have a chat. Jesus got straight to the point and told him he needs to be born again. Then we hit the most famous verse in the Bible: John 3:16. "God so loved the world that he sent his only begotten Son so that whosoever believes in Him will not perish but have eternal life." Charles said, "Jesus loves you so much He came to die on that cross for you, Mike."

All of a sudden a wonderful presence came into the room and I saw that I was turning my back on the one who loved me the most, who hanged on that cross for me. He loved me more than any girl or human being. I cried and cried as I realised that Jesus really was alive and He loved me so much He died on the cross for inferiority-filled, sinful me. After I stopped crying Charles and Eileen led me in a prayer. "Lord Jesus, thank you for dying for my sins on the cross of Calvary. Please forgive me my sins and come into my heart and life, I believe in you, Lord." I felt what was like a great, big rucksack of heavy bricks lifted off my back, I'm sure it was all my sin. I felt elated and light as a feather, full of joy and peace. After a bit more talking and a cup of tea I left their house. I felt so happy and light I was jumping and dancing down the street. I hadn't found a religion or philosophy, I had discovered a wonderful person, the Lord Jesus Christ the Son of God. It really was true that Jesus is alive.

The next day, I was so excited to tell everyone my good news that I had discovered that Jesus really is alive. My enthusiasm was met with exclamations like, "Oh no, Charles has brainwashed him," or "Oh no, Mike's gone all religious." "No, no," I said, "I've found out that Jesus really is alive."

Charles invited me to go with him and others on Saturday night on the streets in Crawley giving out tracts and talking to people. I think I gingerly gave one tract out that night. When I got back to my digs I was told the band had been round to take me to a party. They had never come round to my place before. I later found out that they made a plan to get me onto heroin as a mainliner. If I hadn't met Christ on that Thursday night I'm sure I would have ended up on drugs and most likely died young. If I did anything I put my all into it head on and I'm certain I would have gone for drugs in a big way.

Dear Reader, maybe you have never considered what happens to a person when they die. As you can see from my experience above I hadn't given it much thought either. If you really want to be sure that you will go to Heaven when you die, then pray in faith the following prayer: **Lord Jesus Christ, I thank you for dying on the cross at Calvary for my sin. Thank you**

for taking the punishment for my sin on the cross. Thank you for all that you did on the cross. Please forgive me my sin and come into my heart and life. Please save me and write my name in the book of life. Lord Jesus, I believe in you.

Charles invited me round to his house again to talk about being baptised in water. It was Tuesday the 13th of May 1969 that I knocked on Charles and Eileen's door. They told me about being baptised in water like the early believers did in the New Testament. All this was fine by me: I wanted to do whatever Jesus wanted me to do. Then they opened the Bible at Acts chapters one and two. This is where Jesus in His resurrection body told His disciples to wait in Jerusalem for the Holy Spirit to come. Jesus ascended up into the clouds and the disciples just stared up into the sky. Two men said, "Why are you staring up into the clouds, the same way Jesus has gone into the clouds? He will one day return in the clouds." The followers of Christ waited in an upper room in Jerusalem just as instructed.

When a day called Pentecost had arrived the Holy Spirit came into the upper room like a mighty, loud, rushing wind. Pretty noisy entrance. The believers all had what looked like tongues of fire upon them and they were all filled, or what the Bible calls baptised in the Holy Spirit. Then they all began speaking in foreign languages or tongues by the Holy Spirit. They spilled out into the streets and everyone thought they were drunk, maybe because they looked like drunks and were laughing their heads off and walking funny. After reading the account of this happening after Jesus left planet earth, Charles explained the Holy Spirit is still here today filling believers. Would you like to be filled with the Holy Spirit and speak in tongues? Yes please, I want all that the Lord Jesus has for me. Charles and Eileen laid their hands on me and asked the Holy Spirit to fill me. I was on the floor kneeling on the carpet. I just felt all I can describe as oil going from the top of my head right through my whole body and I began to speak in tongues a language I had never learnt, it just came bubbling out of me. Again I felt even more joy than before and even lighter in my head. It was a wonderful, amazing experience. What this experience did was give me a boldness to talk about Jesus and make Jesus even more real. When we went on the streets of Crawley the following Saturday I gave loads of tracts out and talked to anyone who would listen. We often talked to the rockers and girlfriends about Jesus until one o'clock in the morning in Queens Square. I didn't join a church as such at this time; we met on Wednesday nights to pray for the Saturday night. We called round to see one another in the week to talk about the Lord Jesus and the Bible.

I had moved out of the flats above the shop to live in Langley Green as a lodger. One Wednesday night there was a knock on the door. When I opened the door it was one of the Finnish girl Aila's friends called Vanessa. We called Vanessa 'V' for short, must be the shortest name in history. She said she had a letter from Aila saying that I had become all religious. I had written to Aila explaining my discovery of Jesus. She wrote back saying at her school they were told religion is the opium of the masses. V stood there at the door with a basketful of *The Plain Truth* magazines of her dad's and thought I might like to read them. *The Plain Truth* was the magazine from Herbert W Armstrong, Worldwide Church of God, not for me, I thought. I explained I was just going to a prayer meeting, would you like to join me?

I told her on the way to the prayer meeting my discovery of Jesus. We got down to pray for the Saturday night out on the streets. I heard Charles talk to V and after a while V asked the Lord Jesus to forgive her sins, come into her heart. V was born again and discovered Jesus, too. She was only seventeen and when we went on the streets on a Saturday night she just laughed so much at my silly jokes. Sometimes she was doubled up laughing. I liked V, she was a lovely girl and she loved Jesus. After a few months I got up the courage to ask her out. Before I could ask her out, though, she came to our prayer meeting saying she had met this wonderful man Chris who was in the Navy and was she going out with him. Not long after that V got married at only seventeen. A few years later V came to work in Sainsbury's after travelling around the world with her new husband: sadly she had lost her joy and love for Jesus. One day I will see V in Heaven, I am certain.

At lunchtimes Charles and I sat at the same table to talk about things. He explained there's a meeting in Caxton Hall in London. Peter Scothern was to be the speaker, he is a great man of God. A young student sitting at the table called Ruth interrupted us and said, Can I come? Yes, of course you can, Ruth, we will be leaving Crawley train station at 6.15. About five or six of us went by train to London. We were late; the place was packed. They were singing "What a lovely name, the name of Jesus". The air was electric. Our little group split up and I ended up sitting with Ruth. All of a sudden I started crying, which was puzzling me as I hadn't lost any money or possessions or anything. It was the Holy Spirit crying through me. Peter Scothern stood at the front and said, Right, anyone who wants to be born again come to the front. Next thing I knew Ruth had left me to walk forward to the front. Which was puzzling to me because she had told us she had been going to an Anglican church in Crawley. After everyone had sat down Peter then asked anyone who wanted to be filled with the Holy Spirit to come forward. A crowd of people rushed forward. After everyone had sat down Peter invited anyone who was sick to come to the front. Again a crowd of people rushed forward to be prayed for healing. Then the music started up again full of joy. There were some guys on the stage lay down, rolling back and forth on their sides. I later found out they called them the Holy Rollers. I was really enjoying all this joy and freedom when Ruth tugged on my jumper saying she had to be back home by 10.30 or else she would get into trouble with her dad. "Ok," I said, "I'll take you home, Ruth." I let the others know and off we went. On the way home Ruth was full of joy and was amazed at how the stars and moon looked brighter. Even passing trees and hedges she was just thrilled with creation. Ruth then told me she had been putting tins of Marvel out on the shelves in Sainsbury's and she felt a voice speak to her saying, Marvel not that I say unto you; you must be born again. Which is straight out of John 3, Jesus speaking to Nicodemus. Ruth and I became good friends and she joined our group which we called The Way because that's what the early believers called themselves in the Book of Acts. Ruth was an excellent flautist, classically trained. I would say Ruth's family was middle class, very much into classical music. After a while Ruth's father made Ruth stop coming to our group, The Way: he certainly didn't want his daughter going out with a lowly butcher from Sainsbury's. He had better plans for his daughter. We lost contact with dear Ruth, but whatever happened to her I know that one day I will see her in Heaven, maybe playing the flute.

In The Way we had a guy called Melvyn who used to get really troubled and condemned himself if he hadn't given someone a gospel tract that he had met or seen. One day he was spot on, though: he gave a tract to a guy called John France on the train between East Croydon and Crawley. John worked on the railways and had just finished his shift. The tract was called *The Eternal Question* which struck a chord with John. After they both got off the train at Crawley, Melvyn explained the gospel and prayed with John under a tree just outside the station. John then went to his bedsit and gave his heart and life to the Lord Jesus Christ. John joined our group The Way, too. Glory to Jesus for Melvyn being so obedient. John later on in life became a leader and fine Bible teacher in a Christian fellowship in Bognor Regis and Chichester called Chichester Christian Fellowship. (CCF).

One winter's Saturday night as we were standing on the frosty, icy pavements giving tracts out we prayed. Oh Lord, please warm us up. Then we felt a supernatural warmth come from our feet upwards. God was looking after us while working for Him, keeping us warm. I remember a lady called Lindsay was standing with us at the time who now lives in Bognor Regis running a Bible bookshop called Living Word.

The Salvation Army let us use their hall on a Saturday night for a time. The rockers found out and every Saturday night we had the rockers come to see us. All we gave them was weak coffee or tea and talked about Jesus to them. Some of the rockers were born again and followed Jesus. Some of the lads got mad with us because the girls wouldn't let them have their way with them anymore. After a few months we had to stop our meetings at the Salvation Hall because the congregation didn't like the smell of smoke in the place on a Sunday morning. We moved to a hall on one of the estates in Crawley. Everything was about to change, though, for The Way.

The Way

The Way was growing and new believers like us needed some Bible teaching. Enter a guy called David Moxen, who was an excellent teacher of the Bible and a good pianist and accordion player, too. David held Bible studies for The Way in his house in Crawley.

We still went out on a Saturday night talking to people about Jesus Christ and the way of salvation. One day David gave me the keys to a minibus he had bought for The Way to use. It was a Thames Minibus with enough seats for about ten people in the back. (There were no seat belts in those days.) This was my first vehicle since passing my test, so very exciting for me. David had his own very successful, prosperous printing business. He had some cards printed for us with **THE WAY** on one side, and on the other side an explanation who we were. It went something like this: "The Way are a group of people who have found that Jesus Christ is alive and is who He said He is, the Son of God. They follow His teaching and love to discuss and debate the message of the Gospel of Jesus Christ, why He came and died on the cross."

When we were out on the streets we gave these cards out along with gospel literature we called tracts. All was going really well with The Way: we were seeing people come to know the Lord Jesus.

One day David told us there was a place he would like to take us to in Somerset called South Chard. He told us there was a real move of God's Holy Spirit going on in South Chard and wanted us to experience it. So about ten or twelve of us got into the minibus and I drove us all down to South Chard for the weekend. It took about four hours as I remember. When we arrived we were all shown where we would be sleeping. There was a large house called the Manor House with several small houses or bungalows surrounding it in a horseshoe shape. In the middle of this horseshoe shape of properties was a hall where the meetings took place. We settled into our bedrooms which we shared with complete strangers. We were introduced to a quite large, round lady called Aunty Mill who lived in the Manor House with her very short husband called Uncle Sid. Aunty Mill did all the catering and managed the sleeping arrangements; she had a fine team helping her out. Aunty Mill, I was later to find out, was a great prayer warrior in the Lord. Uncle Sid (Sid Purse) was a wonderful man of God, who was the pastor or leader of the fellowship there. In one of the houses was Harry and Pam Greenwood and family. Uncle Sid and Harry Greenwood used to spend hours praying, waiting on and seeking God along with many others in the fellowship. There was also a fine musician called Andrew Culverwell who went on to make several albums. He later moved to live in the USA where he still lives.

I believe the story of Chard Fellowship in brief goes something like this. Uncle Sid and others waited and sought the Lord for a move of the Holy Spirit. Sid was a builder and built the hall for the fellowship of believers that was growing. After the building had been finished off fully the meetings took place week after week. One day the Lord spoke to Sid to go with a saw and take the lectern down. Which he did and then said, "Where shall I sit now?" The Lord said, "With the congregation." He then remembered the scripture in 1 Corinthians 14:26, which says "When you come together, each one has a song, has a lesson, a revelation, has a tongue, and has an interpretation. Let all these things be done for strengthening the Church." Some of the Church members didn't like this new way of doing things and left. Uncle Sid held onto what the Lord had shown him to do. He even said one day there will be dancing in the church before anything like that had happened in UK churches. The Lord had given him a vision of people dancing in the meetings.

The general format of the meeting developed so that someone would start a song, then another song. The songs were very simple choruses that people received from the Lord straight out of the Bible usually, or based on a revelation they had had. There was no projector showing the words on the wall or a screen. People just memorised the songs and learnt them by heart. Therefore people could close their eyes and concentrate on looking to the Lord. As people worshipped and praised the Lord He gave them a picture, a prophecy, a revelation, a word to share from the Bible, a tongue followed by an interpretation. It was a complete break from Church tradition of two or three hymns, a sermon, then a final hymn and coffee afterwards. It was the Body of Christ sharing with one another as the Holy Spirit moved. Therefore the meetings were called Body Ministry meetings. No one was leading from the front but the mature believers were overseeing what was happening. If someone was talking nonsense or bringing error into the meetings, the leaders would ask them to sit down and correct any wrong teaching. The meetings were full of love, joy, praise, worship and peace. I found them very exciting. Most of all you could feel the tangible presence of the Lord there in the meetings. Jesus said the Father is searching for people who will worship him in spirit and in truth.

We all really enjoyed this way of having a meeting with such freedom in the Holy Spirit. When we arrived back at Crawley we began to have meetings in our homes based on what we had learnt in Chard. At that time in the early 70s there were a large number of Christians meeting in homes, breaking away from traditional meetings. This became known as the house group movement. There was a move of the Holy Spirit in the Anglican churches also, which was aptly named the Renewal. Some traditional churches were against this move of the Holy Spirit saying such things as speaking in tongues is of the Devil, the gifts of the Holy Spirit finished long ago. There are nine gifts of the Holy Spirit taught in 1 Corinthians chapter twelve. Gift of tongues, interpretation of tongues, prophecy, a word of knowledge, a word of wisdom, discernment, healing, miracles and faith. To describe each one of these gifts would take too long in this passage. There are plenty of books and teaching on the gifts of the Holy Spirit, but believe me they are all functioning today in the Body of Christ.

I used to help David Moxen run an afternoon Sunday school in Uckfield. One day we called in to see a couple called Simon and Joyce Short, who lived in Newick, and who had also been to South Chard Fellowship. They ran a small house group in their lovely, large home. We were welcomed in and given a cup of tea and chatted away about what amazing things were happening in Chard. Then they said, "Let's just have a pray before we go on our way." While we prayed my heart was pumping fast as the Holy Spirit was upon me and in my mind these words were churning around. I spoke out the words that were churning around in my mind. Joyce then said, "That was a prophecy!" I had my first prophecy from the Holy Spirit there and then: it has been the gift that God has used me in the most ever since that time.

We carried on having wonderful house group meetings with the occasional visit from someone from Chard like a guy called Tony Nash. I played the guitar, leading praise and worship as the songs were pretty simple choruses and easy to play. We also continued for a while going out on the streets talking to people about Jesus and the gospel. After a while we stopped going out on the streets which now, looking back, I think we should have carried on doing. David Moxen had enquired on my behalf about me getting into an Assembly of God Bible College at Kenley in Surrey. I was accepted but at some time when I was visiting South Chard again Uncle Sid and Ian Andrews advised I would have to unlearn a lot of what they taught. I would have come out of the college with some sort of qualification and given a small congregation to pastor, I guess. God had other plans for my life. I remember saying to the Lord, If I can't go to Bible school I want to join the School of the Holy Spirit. Jesus talked about Him leaving the earth and sending the Holy Spirit: He will guide you and lead you into all truth. The Holy Spirit is a person, a part of the Godhead, not a force or power.

Sainsbury's decided to move me to the Purley branch which was about a 30-minute drive in the minibus. I continued to meet at Crawley with The Way.

I lived above the shop in Purley, as was the trend for Sainsbury's in those days. I shared a room with another employee at the store who worked in the grocery section. One morning he was really mad at me saying I had woken him up at three o'clock in the morning. I said, "How had I woken him up at three o'clock in the morning?" He said that I had sat bolt upright in bed with my arms high in the air and shouted "Hallelujah!" at the top of my voice. I had no recollection of doing such a thing. I did hear once that your spirit is always worshipping God even if you are not aware of it yourself. King David, who wrote a lot of the Psalms, often says, Bless the Lord oh my soul, which some say he is telling his soul off saying, Come on, bless the Lord, soul! I think we still need to do that today. Our flesh wars against the spirit. A few weeks later I was given a single room right at the top of the building that was really meant for assistant managers. I was getting closer to Heaven, I guess!

It was now November time and I still hadn't been baptised in water so David Moxen organised a date. The date came round: it was freezing cold and snowing. I drove to Crawley and picked up a few people in the minibus and followed David in his estate car. The snow got worse; I could just see his tail lights in front of me. I had no idea where we were going: it seemed to take ages. We arrived at Paddock Wood in Kent, I think it was Arthur Burt's church hall. The church hall was really warm and the baptismal tank ready and thankfully warmed up, too. David played his accordion and we sang and praised the Lord. I was duly baptised along with others in the name of Jesus. At that time South Chard taught that there were more scriptures saying baptise in the name of Jesus Christ than the one scripture that says baptise in the name of the Father, Son and Holy Ghost. The word 'baptise' in Greek means "to be identified with and plunged into". It was Christ who died and rose again, not the Father or the Holy Spirit. Being baptised into Christ meant you were being identified with his death and burial and resurrection from the grave. It was taught that you were burying your old self (old man) and rising to a new life in Christ. Some say the scripture in Matthew was meant for the believers in the great seven-year tribulation. Much of the Gospel of Matthew can be related to Israel. The debate goes on to this day. At this point if you are disturbed about such teaching, reach for your Bible concordance and Bible and research with an open mind and heart to what is actually written.

I drove back to Crawley and dropped everyone off then went back to the Purley store to my room at the top of Sainsbury's. It was now one o'clock in the morning but I felt so alive and full of life and energy! I knelt down for a time of prayer and I felt a wonderful, powerful anointing of the Holy Spirit filling me with so much love and joy I could burst. About an hour later I jumped into my bed and slept like a baby. As time went on I found the pull of the worldly things just fell away. I had no desire to go to dances or to see bands anymore, I just wanted more and more of Jesus in my life.

I had been dating a very pretty student girl who had come to work at the store. My friends said the relationship wouldn't work as she didn't know the Lord. I tried to get her to believe in the Lord Jesus but she didn't want to know, so I ended the relationship and from there on I was only going to go out with girls who were believers. Later in the year I went to Chard for the weekend and I overheard someone sharing about baptism in water. They were saying that if you are not baptised in water it's like the children of Israel at the Red Sea. They were being led out of Egypt following the ten plagues, then the Egyptians decided to go after them. There was just a cloud separating Israel from the pursuing Egyptians: they were trapped. God said to Moses, Stretch out your rod over the Red Sea. The sea opened up, a mighty wind blew and dried the sea bottom, and the next day they crossed over on dry ground with a wall of water on either side of them. The Egyptians went in after the Israelites but Moses raised his staff again and God closed the Red Sea back over them. They never saw the Egyptians again.

Egypt in the Bible represents many times the world system with Pharaoh being likened to the Devil. The Israelites were cut off from the world of the Egyptians, so when you are baptised you are cut off from the world: your old way of living like a slave with taskmasters has gone! I suddenly realised that that had been my experience when I was baptised a few months earlier. This revelation was so real to me that I wanted to be baptised again to do it properly. I even embarrassed myself by going forward at a baptism meeting that weekend to be baptised again. Uncle Sid said, No, no, you don't need to be baptised again, and asked Harry Greenwood to take me out of the meeting and minister to me.

He took me to his house, Miracle, and explained I had come into the revelation of what had happened to me and what I was in. Harry then gave me a prophecy which I have held onto for the rest of my life. It went something like this: You shall have many giants in your life, but you will be like David. You shall go to the stream of God's Holy Spirit and get a stone which is a word from God. You shall sling the stone of God's Word at the giant like David slung the stone at Goliath. The giant will fall and you will do what David did, take the sword and cut off the giant's head. Take the sword of the Spirit and destroy the giant. The story of David and Goliath has always been precious to me: there is such a lot to learn about spiritual warfare in the passage that tells of David and Goliath. The prophecy that Harry gave me has been so true in my life. I have had many giants to deal with and most of them have been dealt with. Some giants haven't fallen and I don't know why, only God knows. David took five stones from the stream to kill Goliath. I have learnt that the number five speaks of grace. It was the Grace of God that delivered Israel from being defeated. King Saul's heavy armour and sword didn't help David beat Goliath. It speaks of the natural way of doing things to beat our giants. God has a way to beat your giant today: ask him for a stone, a word from the Holy Spirit to defeat your giant today. It's interesting that when David approached the battle lines and Goliath came out defying Israel's God, David said, "Who is this uncircumcised Philistine, that he defies the armies of the living God?" In other words we have a covenant with God; these Philistines don't have a covenant with God. It was much later on that I was to discover the power of the covenant relationship that I have with the Lord.

I used to go for weekends to South Chard Fellowship. I went to South Chard for a week's holiday one particular time, travelling by train from London. The carriages were different in the 1970s to today's carriages. Each carriage had its own compartment with two bench-type seats either side. The seats were very bouncy, soft and comfy as the train ambled along. I was reading a Watchman Nee book, *Sit, Walk, Stand*, based on scriptures from Ephesians. The first chapter was basically saying Christianity in one's life begins by realising Christ has done it all for us on the cross and by His resurrection from the dead. When

He said, "It is finished," he meant **it is finished**, he had accomplished full salvation for those who believe and trust in Him. It says we are seated in heavenly places in Christ Jesus, hence the first chapter is named, Sit. As I travelled along this bouncy, comfy train carriage, the revelation that I was seated with Christ in heavenly places hit me. I can't do anything to earn God's favour. Christ has done it all for me and He now sees me in Christ: it's by God's grace that I have been saved. Such peace and joy entered my heart and mind: by the end of the journey I was on cloud nine. Aunty Mill collected me from Axminster station to take me to South Chard. I had a wonderful time in Somerset seeing the sites. On a Wednesday night they had the midweek meeting, then again on Saturday and Sunday. I must explain at this time I was in my early twenties, full of life and energy. When I went to meetings I would praise, shout and worship the Lord loudly, as I have a loud voice. If I did anything I did it with everything I've got, full bore. When it came to the Saturday night meeting I was asked to sit outside the meeting on the bench seat just outside the manor house kitchen door. They didn't want me to go into the meeting. At the time I didn't know why but on reflection now, I think it was because I was too loud! I sat on the seat longingly watching the congregation praising, worshipping, dancing before the Lord through the church windows.

All of a sudden I felt someone physically sit by me,

I felt his hip and leg next to mine, his arm around my shoulder and he hugged me. I nestled my head into His chest. It felt like Jesus, it may have been an angel, I don't know. However, I do know that I had a wonderful time outside the meeting being loved by the Lord, on the seat by the kitchen door. We sing – "Isn't the love of Jesus simply wonderful, wonderful...? Praise his holy name." Praise the lovely Lord Jesus, He's the lover of my soul. Wonderful Jesus! His love is higher than the highest mountains, deeper than the deepest sea, wider than the widest ocean. It says: **See what great love the Father has lavished on us, that we should be called children of God! And that's what we are! 1 John 3:1**.

At this particular time there was a strong feeling that communism would take over the United Kingdom. We had heard about the Christians in communist countries being persecuted through Pastor Wurmbrand, who wrote *Tortured for Christ*. We knew through Brother Andrew's book, *God's Smuggler*, about the persecution and the confiscation of Bibles, therefore the need to get Bibles into these countries. There was a book going round called Vanjah, a brother who was persecuted. The prison officers took a jug of water and a dog into the prison cell. They poured water into a dish and dog lapped it up and five minutes later it was dead because of arsenic in the water. Then from the same jug they gave Vanjah water in a glass to drink. They were waiting for him to keel over and die, he didn't. They were testing the verse in Mark 16 where Jesus said you shall drink any deadly poison and it will not harm you. The prison officers walked out full of anger. Another time they stood Vanjah outside where it was 30 degrees below freezing with just his pyjamas on. They had to keep rotating the guards but the Lord kept Vanjah warm. It was hearing these stories that gave me a desire not to give into any persecution even ready by God's grace to die for Christ. I was sold out to Jesus, He meant everything to me, I had abandoned the dance halls and worldly pleasures, and I wanted to do God's will. This may seem like having an unhappy life to some but at that time I was full of the joy of the Lord. We used to sing – Be filled with the Spirit, speaking to yourselves in Psalms and hymns and spiritual songs, singing and making melody in your hearts to the Lord. Straight out of the Bible.

Looking back now I think they were probably some of the happiest times in my life being completely sold out to Jesus. Apostle Paul said if you are single you seek to please the Lord; if you are married you seek to please your wife. Later, I found that to be the case, although at the time I thought that wouldn't happen to me: Jesus is first. You could say I was fanatical at this time about Jesus and His Kingdom. Jesus said, "Seek first the Kingdom of God and his righteousness and all these things will be added unto you" (speaking of material possessions). I did my very best to seek His

Kingdom first. We had been taught about giving by Harry Greenwood, that tithing was an Old Testament law or temple tax. Everything we have belongs to the Lord. Ideally we give as led by the Holy Spirit as and when He requires the money or possession we have. Tithing isn't mentioned in the New Testament as far as I can see; instead, the early believers sold any spare property and possessions they had and distributed them to those in need. I do not read anywhere in the Book of Acts where they gathered money for a building. At this time I used to sometimes give half my wages away to different ministries or people in the Body of Christ. As long as I had clothes and food I was content. Jesus said, "A man's life consists not in the abundance of the things which he possesses". I used to cringe at some of the meetings in Westminster Central Hall in London, where the visiting preacher would put pressure on people to give. One guy used to say things like, "I feel the Holy Spirit is saying – the figure you have just thought about giving, now double it." The only thing is he used to say the same thing at every meeting.

I used to hear stories of Uncle Sid and Harry Greenwood fasting and waiting on God for hours on end, sitting at Jesus's feet. Jesus went to see Mary and Martha one day. Martha was busy doing things round the house but Mary just sat at Jesus's feet talking to Him. Martha got upset but Jesus said, "One thing is needful: Mary has chosen that good part, which shall not be taken away from her." Jesus said, "When you pray go into your closet and shut the door and your heavenly Father, that sees in secret, shall reward you openly." With all this in mind I used to go into my bedroom, close the door and put my watch on the bed, thinking I am going to time myself for one hour of prayer. As I knelt before the King of Kings to spend one hour in prayer I found after ten minutes thoughts crowded my mind of things I should be doing, rather than waste time praying! I stayed down on my knees the whole hour determined to seek the Lord. After about 50 minutes I broke through into the Lord's presence then the hour was up: off to work or bed. After a year or so of doing this I found the time became shorter and shorter before I broke into God's presence. It was probably 30 minutes. Keeping up this devotional time, after a few years it was fifteen minutes before I felt the presence of the Lord. It remained that way for some years. Nowadays it only takes me five or ten minutes to experience His presence and filling of the Holy Spirit and now time just goes by really fast as I am taken up with Jesus mostly. There was at that time a little book by a monk it was called *The Practice of the Presence of God*. The monk just kept in mind and heart God is with me, He is near in the busiest of times in the kitchen or wherever. God is of course always with us, we just have to tune into Him. I have had some wonderful times practising the presence of God. After all He is in me! Driving my car speaking in tongues and praising the Lord of Lords, He has spoken to me so clearly in such times. Waiting on the Lord and spending time with Him is not fashionable these days, I feel. In meetings where we are waiting on God there is usually someone plucking a guitar or playing the keyboard. It is as if silently waiting on God is so hard for anyone to do.

On one Saturday's news there was a report of a rally in Trafalgar Square put on by the Nationwide Festival of Light in September 1971. Among the main speakers were Mary Whitehouse, Lord Longford and Malcolm Muggeridge, all campaigning for more censorship on TV programmes and films. They were against all the violence and explicit sexual content in the media. I remember Julia McKenzie was singing, too. I had watched Malcolm Muggeridge several times on the TV, usually a late-night programme debating current issues of society. I just thought, after watching the rally in London, that I would like to meet Malcolm Muggeridge. I was still working for Sainsbury's where we always had Mondays off with every fourth Saturday off. I knew from watching TV that he lived in or near Robertsbridge, so on the Monday after the rally I set off to find Malcolm.

When I reached Robertsbridge I asked various people where Malcolm Muggeridge lived. After following directions, I ended up on a farm track leading to a large cottage in the middle of a field. I gingerly knocked on the door and Malcolm answered it. I asked him if he was Malcolm Muggeridge, and he replied that he was.

"Hello, I'm Mike. I've come to see you," I said.

Instead of slamming the door shut, he said, "My dear boy, come in," and he asked his wife, Kitty, to make a cup of tea. I explained I had seen him at the rally and wanted to meet him. I then went on and told them both the story of how I had found Christ and explained about the small group I belonged to called The Way. He was fascinated to hear my story, how I had met the Lord Jesus and we both talked about Him. Malcolm was full of Jesus and His love, so kind and patient. From that time on we became friends, occasionally meeting up, but mostly keeping in touch by letters. I believe Malcolm changed from being an Anglican to a Catholic, as he felt they kept closer to the Word of God on morals. Many would disagree with his move and thoughts about the Catholic faith. I think he was greatly influenced by meeting Mother Teresa of Calcutta, who went out to the poorest of the poor and took in the dying off the streets and gave them a place in her buildings to die with dignity. Both Mother Teresa and Malcolm shone with the presence and light of the Holy Spirit. I did hear once that Malcolm said he used to lie on his bed and feel his spirit hovering over his body then coming back in. I guess one day his spirit was hovering over his body and then off he flew to Heaven. I know that Malcolm is in Heaven and one day I will see him again. Who knows, I may go up to his mansion and knock on his door and say, "Hello, I'm Mike."

I continued to work at Sainsbury's Purley store. The other butchers called me The Reverend because I talked about Jesus all the time. One Saturday afternoon when it was really quiet in the store. I was just tidying up in the refrigerator and cutting up some meat at the block. Suddenly the three butchers in their thirties came into the room squirting one another with water pistols. One of them squirted me with some water. So I calmly went to the sink and began to fill a bucket with water. Two of the lads saw what I intended to do while the lad closest to me said, "No, The Reverend wouldn't do that." The Reverend did just that and poured the bucket of water all over his head. He just stood there in utter shock and unbelief. The other two laughed their heads off. From there on in I was able to share about Jesus having some deep conversations as we worked together. I think the water bucket incident showed them Christians can have fun, too.

One day I had a fever and was full of cold. I was really blocked up so much so I could hardly talk. I remember at night kneeling at my bed and just saying the only word I could utter, "Lord", about half an hour. Suddenly I knew Jesus was in the room. He touched my head the fever left me instantly and my head cleared. I got into bed and slept to awake the next day at six o'clock bright as a button. Normally with such a heavy cold I would be off work for a few days. Then I read the scripture: "those who call on the Name of The Lord shall be saved". The word 'saved' in the original Greek means made whole. God was teaching me in the School of the Spirit about divine healing.

Sainsbury's opened a new store in Crawley just near the old store in Queens Square. I asked if I could move back to work in the new store. Permission granted, I moved to live in lodgings with Mrs Karcha in Langley Green. Mrs Karcha was a wonderful lady who cooked great meals and did all my washing. She had a daughter and husband that attended an Anglican church in Crawley. We had some interesting conversations. It was exciting working in the new Sainsbury's store. They introduced some new ways of working which made it easier for us butchers. I continued to talk about Jesus at any given opportunity. The Way was growing. I was still strumming out praise and worship songs on my guitar: all was well.

I didn't have much to do on a Saturday night now we had stopped going on the streets. I made some friends of some youngsters like myself who attended a youth group. It was based in the Anglican church. They had a guy and his girlfriend who was very enthusiastic about dance drama. The youth group put on some very powerful productions using dance to proclaim the gospel message. They once did C.S.

Lewis's *Screwtape Letters*, depicting the battle of good and evil. I made a great impact on them, I think: they used to call me 'Praise the Lord Mike Davis'. I introduced them to books by Watchman Nee, Kathryn Kuhlman, and the like. Once a cassette tape came my way with a message on it by Ern Baxter which I shared with this youth group. The message influenced my walk with the Lord in a big way. It was all about how God's creatures speak to us by illustration. Ern had chosen to talk on eagles and how they illustrate how God would like us to live and walk with the Lord. He was saying that first there are two types of eagles in the Bible, the imperial and the golden eagle. Imperial speaks of our standing in Christ as kings and priests unto God. Golden speaks to us how precious we are in Him, bought not with silver and gold but with the precious blood of Christ. This eagle builds its nest high up in the mountains: we have a high calling. The little eaglets grow up in a nice, comfy nest. Mum and Dad bring in the food: all is well.

When we are first saved and are babes in Christ all seems so comfy. One day the little eaglets thinks Mum's gone crazy because she starts breaking up the nest, leaving them standing on the edge of the mountain. Then she pushes one of the eaglets off the edge and it goes tumbling down, squawking, thinking this its life's over. Just as eaglet is about to hit the ground Mum comes sweeping under it and takes it on her back to the top of the cliff and does it all over again. About the sixth time going down little eaglet remembers what Mum did just before she broke up the nest and went crazy. She hovered over the nest using her big wings and the little eaglet thought, What big wings you've got, Mum. Little eaglet thinks on the way down: I've got two wings, I'll stick them out and see what happens. So eaglet learns to fly. We have two wings spiritually, one of praise and the other of prayer. When difficult times come along we are instructed to pray with thanksgiving. Philippians 4: Rejoice in the Lord always and again I say Rejoice… Do not be anxious about anything, but in every situation by prayer and petition, with thanksgiving, present your requests to God, and the peace of God which transcends all understanding, will guard your hearts and minds in Christ Jesus.

God teaches us to use our wings of praise and prayer as we grow up in Him. He reveals how strong and mighty He is: we can trust in Him. The eagle waits on a rock and waits for the right thermal of air to come along. When it does he lets out a yell of delight and gets carried up higher and higher by the thermal. In Isaiah 40 it says they that wait upon the Lord shall renew their strength, they will soar on wings like eagles, they shall run and not grow weary and they will walk and not faint. That's what the Lord wants believers to do, wait on Him for the thermal of the Holy Spirit to take them up higher and higher. The Eagle has two sets of eyelids: one ordinary pair, then another thinner pair which he pulls down as he gets higher, so he can look at the sun through these thinner eyelids. God wants us to soar higher and higher looking at the Son (Sun of righteousness) of God, Jesus. It says if we draw close to God, He will draw close to us and we are made near unto God by the blood of Christ. We have the means to gaze into the face of our saviour. We sing: Turn your eyes upon Jesus, look full in His wonderful face, and the things of earth will grow strangely dim, in the light of His glory and grace.

When eagles get sick they find a high rock and lie on it, letting the sun make them better. When we get sick physically or spiritually we rest on the Rock Jesus Christ and let His presence heal us. Times of refreshing from the presence of the Lord. I love the presence of the Lord. When an eagle gets to about 40 he gets alone and starts pulling out his worn-out feathers and his blunt talons. Then he smashes his beak because it's worn and blunt. Then he waits until new feathers, talons and beak are grown back out and he lives another 40 years.

Psalm 103: Praise the Lord, My soul and forget not all His benefits – who forgives all your sins, and heals all your diseases, who redeems your life from the pit and crowns you with love and compassion, satisfies your desires with good things **so that your youth is renewed like the eagles.**

Today I pray, renew my youth like the eagles, Lord!

There is much more about eagles but this message by Ern Baxter gave me the desire to be an eagle Christian and live and walk close to God, soar into His presence. I wanted to be and still want to be an eagle-type Christian. There are other birds that God uses to illustrate messages, like the crow who hops around on the ground, not soaring much. You get Christians who don't like soaring into God's presence, just happy to hop around in life relying on their own strength and intellect. The ostrich who buries his head in the sand so that no one will see him. The lemmings who follow one another, even to running over the edge of a cliff to certain death. Jesus said… that broad is the road that leads to destruction, and there are many that go down it.

Our little group The Way was asked to pray for a man called John King. His marriage had broken up and he wasn't in a good place. As we prayed the Lord gave someone a picture of a black heart turning white. We didn't know he was a backslidden Christian and had not been at all good to his wife, even wanting to kill her. After we had prayed we found out God had visited him and he prayed Psalm 51 which is a psalm of repentance that David wrote after his affair with Bathsheba. I went to see John and we became good friends, although he was older than me. We had some great times of fellowship talking through what the Bible teaches. We heard there was a fellowship in Chichester that met on a Tuesday night at the Bassil

Shippam Centre, the Chichester Christian Fellowship, which was into Body Ministry like Chard. John and I used to go along on a Tuesday night: it was the highlight of our week. The meetings were powerful, full of God's presence: as usual no agenda, we just began singing and praising the Lord using choruses we all knew by heart. Then someone would share a word or prophecy, see a picture, by the end of the evening a message had come through from the Holy Spirit. Very precious times full of the joy and presence of the Holy Spirit.

I was still working at Sainsbury's store in Crawley. One day I was really sick with vomiting and diarrhoea and was told to go home and get better. I was off work for three days. About a month later, I was at the store working on the refrigerated counters. My temperature went up and I began feeling sick again. This time, though, I put into practice what I had been taught about confessing the Word of God in faith. For about an hour I confessed all the scriptures on healing, like By His stripes you were healed, or I am the Lord who heals you. Gradually my temperature went down and feeling sick just left me. I didn't have any time off work: the Holy Spirit was teaching me how powerful it is to confess God's Word.

I used to go back to see my parents at least twice a year. They had moved from Lincoln back to their roots. They now lived in a council flat in Tattershall. While visiting Lincolnshire I used to seek out any

Christian fellowship near to Tattershall. I heard about a meeting held in a hamlet called Branston Booths in the village hall. I managed to find it one Sunday night but was late going into the meeting. I always took my guitar wherever I went. Seeing I was late I quickly sat down in the only seat I could see which was in the front row. We sang some hymns and the preacher preached his sermon, another hymn and the meeting ended.

I was approached after the meeting and asked if I would like a cup of tea. Yes please, I replied. They thought I was with the visiting speaker. After a while they found out I wasn't with the visiting preacher, and a young man called Ken came over to me, asking about my guitar in its case. He encouraged me to get my guitar out, and the next thing I knew I was teaching them some choruses. Afterwards, Ken invited me to visit him and his wife Pam in Lincoln. When I went to see them we never stopped talking about the Lord and things of the Kingdom of God. I met their daughter Susan and son Craig. Ken and Pam used to go to a couple's house in Welton, just outside Lincoln on a Tuesday night. If I was staying in Lincolnshire longer than a weekend I would go to the house group there, too. Ken and Pam have been my very special friends ever since. Little did I know that this connection was going to be important in the next stage of my life.

Back Home

My time in Crawley, I felt, was coming to an end, as my father's health was getting worse. I decided to move back home to be with my parents. I felt I would like to do something between leaving my job at Sainsbury's and going back home. I had heard about an organisation called Operation Mobilisation (OM), whose founder was George Verwer. Every year, over the summer period, OM went on a mission covering Europe, spreading the Gospel of Jesus Christ. I applied to OM to go to Belgium on a mission trip.

I left Sainsbury's much to my manager's puzzlement, giving up my career with the company. Some employees gave their whole heart and life up working for Sainsbury's. It was almost like the company was their god.

I arrived in a place called Zaventem and was taken to a big, old building that used to be a seminary. I was told which room I was to sleep in, but when I got to the room there was no bed. I went back to the desk and informed them there were no beds. I was sent to the pile of cardboard in the hallway and told to use it as a padding to sleep on in my sleeping bag. Oh, ok, I thought.

We had a week of prayer and teaching before being sent to our various countries. I think there were about four or five hundred of us from all over Europe. We all got together at ten o'clock after breakfast for two hours of prayer. The person at the front led the prayer time by sharing a specific need in a particular country. We were in groups of ten or fifteen and prayed about the need. Sometimes the need was for protection against the enemy attacking the mission. After lunch, George Verwer taught us in the afternoon meetings about evangelism. In the evenings we praised and worshipped God and had more teaching, and there was more sharing about what was happening in various countries. After a week of doing this the place was like Heaven on earth. The presence of the Lord was so strong and our unity was so great. We then all got sent to our various towns or cities across Europe to spread the gospel, the good news of Jesus Christ.

I was sent to a town in Belgium where there was a very large barge called The Ark. It was moored on one of the big canals. Every day after breakfast we had prayer and some more instruction on the day's proceedings. I couldn't speak French or Flemish so had to pray for English-speaking visitors to the Ark to talk about Jesus. Every day the Lord would send people I could talk to, and it was amazing. I was on the Ark about three to four weeks with the team. We saw quite a number of people come to know the Lord. I met and worked with some wonderful people who were sold out for the Lord Jesus. I found it a very exciting time.

After OM I moved in with my parents in Tattershall into the small bedroom in their flat. My father's lung cancer was getting worse, so it was good for me to be home to support my mum. My sister Janet was living in Coningsby and it was nice seeing my sister on a regular basis. My brother and his wife Ivy were living in Lincoln, so I could see them more regularly, too. There wasn't a job in the meat trade, so I obtained a job at RAF Coningsby working in the officers' mess as a cleaner. I used to start at seven o'clock in the morning and finish at three-thirty in the afternoon. It was a fill-in job, just to get me by until something better came along. It meant I had lots of free time to read and go out to meetings in the evenings.

During this time I still kept in touch with South Chard Fellowship. They held a conference one year in the Chard town hall which I attended. The speakers were Harry Greenwood, Derek Prince, Ian Andrews and Uncle Sid (as I remember). I loved Harry's ministry, especially inspirational on faith and hearing the Lord: his ministry really blessed my life. Derek ministered one afternoon about Zion, it was something like a three- or four-hour Bible study that just seemed like an hour. I still remember the message about when the Lord set the people free from Babylon to return to Zion in Jerusalem – we used to sing a song about it – when the Lord turned again the captivity of Zion we were like those that dreamed…

At the conference there was opportunity to have prayer for healing. My lower back was in pain mainly due to my very physical job on my feet all day lifting and stretching. I went for prayer and Derek sat me on a chair and measured one leg against the other. One leg was about an inch shorter than the other. He prayed and I physically felt my leg lengthen, it was amazing. Yes, my back was better, but rather puzzling, I have since that time had prayer for back problems over the years and again my legs were different lengths, and again I felt the leg grow each time. I sometimes joke about all this leg lengthening, saying before I became a Christian I was only five feet two. Last time I measured my height I was six feet one. Uncle Sid had a strong deliverance ministry and it wasn't unusual to hear demons screaming out of people as in the Book of Acts. Ian Andrews ministered in the Holy Spirit and we saw miracles and healings. It was a really wonderful time, full of love, joy and peace in the Holy Spirit. I shall never forget it.

After being in Lincolnshire for a few months I discovered what was going on church-wise. I was involved with three house groups in Lincolnshire. One was on a Tuesday night at Welton, twenty-three miles away, meeting with Ken and Pam and friends. Another was in the officers' quarters in Coningsby, at Humph and Lynn's house, on a Wednesday night. Then, finally, I met on a Friday night in Arthur and Muriel's house at Ruskington, near Sleaford, which was about seventeen miles away. All three house group meetings were different in the way they ran and the numbers of people. The common denominator was all the people were hungry for more of God and loved the Lord Jesus. I used to take my guitar to each meeting to lead the praise and worship. The presence of the Lord was so evident and the gifts of the Holy Spirit flowed. In Humph and Lynn's house group we used to have people on a short visit of only a few months, staying at the RAF station on a course. If they hadn't been baptised, we used to baptise them in the bath as there was plenty of room in the officers' quarters' bathrooms. If they hadn't been baptised in the Holy Spirit, we used to pray for them to receive the Holy Spirit. I think over a two- or three-year period we had about two hundred people through the house group. One of the officers, Gordon, and his wife, had a bungalow in Tattershall Thorpe and wanted me to look after it while they were away for two years or so. The bungalow was called Pippins, as there used to be Cox's Orange Pippins grown in that area the bungalow was on.

My time at Pippins was great, as it was quiet and the place had three bedrooms which meant I could invite friends to stay. Also I could hold meetings of my own there, too. There was a fireplace, so I could have log fires in the winter. Across the lane was a farmer and his wife whom I made friends with. They reared a beef herd and on one occasion I butchered a whole carcase for them for their freezer. Very nice people.

I heard of a job going at George Adams meat-processing factory in Ruskington. I applied and got the job working on the boning line. George Adams, a Spalding-based company, was famous in the area for making sausages, pork pies, faggots,scotch eggs and plumb loaf. This job meant standing at a butcher's table boning out pork all day long. We started at 7am and finished at 5.30pm. It sounds a tough job but the days just flew by so fast. It was while I was at George Adams that my father died of cancer at the young age of 64 years. I was numb with grief for about a month or so but the Lord was with me, His presence was round me like a big bubble. After a while, though, I thought back to when I first started butchering, about the Meat Inspector coming in to inspect the meat at J R Goose in his pressed clean, white coat. I thought, "That's what I want to do." I wrote to colleges at Smithfield, Ipswich and Manchester enquiring about meat inspection training courses. One day the Lord just spoke to my heart direct, saying Manchester. The Smithfield and Ipswich colleges wrote back saying, Sorry, we don't do that course anymore. Then through the post came a letter from Manchester Polytechnic asking me to attend an interview. I made contact with a Christian fellowship in Redditch I had heard about and arranged to stay with them. The pastor Duggie Reid took me to the interview and I was offered a place to study for a Meat Inspection and other qualifications they did. I arranged to live in one of Duggie's flats above the meeting room. I found the whole thing very exciting. In those days one could get a grant to live on as well as free tuition.

I arrived at Hollings College in Manchester in September 1975. I was given a place at a United Reformed Church College hall of residence in Whalley Range. Whalley Range was a red-light district in Manchester at that time. I liked living in the United Reformed Theological College halls of residence, as it was so different to any other place I had lived in before. My bedroom was on the first floor. It was about fourteen feet by eight feet, oblong, with a window overlooking the grounds, grass and trees. There was a bed, wardrobe, chest of drawers and a desk, and everything I needed to do my studies. I felt so thankful for my lovely room and the adventure I was on.

The guy in the room opposite to mine was studying to be a theologian for the United Reformed Church. Over the year, I had some conversations with him about the Bible. I felt, in the end, he only believed in about a quarter or less of what the Bible actually said. The Red Sea became the Reed Sea: that's how the children of Israel could pass over the sea. Many such explanations to dissolve the miraculous Acts of God.

Hollings College at this time was a polytechnic on Wilmslow Road in Manchester which ran various courses such as art, textiles, food science, as well as meat technology. I soon got into the swing of daily life at Hollings, starting at 8am and finishing at 5pm, having lectures on microbiology, parasitology, meat production, company law, specific diseases, nutrition, and biology and meat inspection. Later on, we used to go to Manchester abattoir to see first-hand the process of meat inspection and view diseased carcases and organs. The lecturers were very interesting to listen to, with their vast knowledge on their particular subjects. One or two guys stood out, like the man who taught us parasitology. He used to come in holding about four or five large books all over three inches thick. He knew his subject inside out, telling us the life cycle of a particular parasite and its various hosts. We joked about some of the parasites whose whole purpose in their life was to copulate then die – what a way to go! After a day of lectures at Hollings, I travelled back to my hall of residence. At 6.30pm the bell rang out, calling us to dinner in the large dining hall, furnished with long tables with seats either side. After grace was said, we all tucked into the dish of the day. I can't remember having any bad meals at the halls of residence. The meals were accompanied by interesting conversation with students from all different backgrounds studying all kinds of subjects.

Dinner usually ended at 7.30pm to 8pm, after which I went straight to my room to go over the day's lectures or write an essay. I had to learn these strange names of all the bacteria or parasites and how to pronounce them, too. I usually carried on studying until midnight, stretching my brain like never before. As well as all this, I kept up my devotional life of prayer, praise and reading the Bible. It was a very precious and wonderful time.

On a Wednesday nights, I went to the Redditch Christian Fellowship, taking my guitar and sometimes prophesying or sharing a word from the scriptures. The meetings started at 8pm and finished about 10-10.30pm all in the form of Body Ministry, where we never knew what God was going to say to us. The meetings were full of praise, worship and manifestations of the gifts of the Holy Spirit. Doug Reid was very good at training people how to hear God and move in the gifts of the Holy Spirit. All the meetings were very exciting, full of people who wanted more of God in their lives, wanting to walk closer to Him. We sometimes had visitors like Arthur Burt or Ian Andrews, which was brilliant. I loved when Arthur Burt walked into the meeting and shared Holy Spirit-anointed truth. He had some sayings that have stuck with me like these:

When the shaker starts shaking, get into the shaker and you won't be shaken.

Lots of Christians have lemons hidden in their

cupboards but what a wonderful day when God shows how to make lemonade. (In other words, sweet forgiveness instead of bitterness.)

Meetings are like shop windows: you see something you would like, but it's out there in the world. You get the funds to buy it. The Bible says Buy the truth and sell it not.

When Ian came we had healing and miracles along with superb teaching on moving in the Holy Spirit.

I also went to the meetings on a Saturday night, Sunday morning and evening. On Sundays, I used to go to Doug's house in Lea Road where the people living there cooked a lovely meal. We all had some great times of fellowship sharing our experiences of walking with Jesus. After a while, I found out I could hear the Lord's voice so clearly. Jesus said, "My sheep hear my voice." I can only put this down to my mind being exercised and stretched by studying so much. Some cults, on the other hand, teach to empty one's mind and repeat a mantra, for example. From this experience, I feel, studying and using one's mind is of great assistance to having a closer walk with God. Of course the best thing one can study is the Word of God, the Bible.

My life carried on in this vein for a whole ten months, then the time came for all the exams. Right at the start of my move to Manchester to study, the Lord had given me, several times in several ways, a promise from the Bible. It was Isaiah 41:10: **Fear not**

for I am with you, do not be dismayed, for I am your God, I will strengthen you and help you; I will uphold you with my righteous right hand. One thing I feared was exams because I had always done very badly in exams at school. Here, the word that God had given me helped me greatly. It was like a stone to kill the giant of inferiority, and for me to say, with God's help, I can pass these exams.

We had three qualifications of exams to take; the first was six three-hour papers with three ten-minute oral examinations in front of two qualified meat inspectors and one Environmental Health Office (EHO). Then there was another exam of six three-hour papers. The final exam for meat inspection itself was taken at Liverpool, for some reason. It was a two-hour written paper with three ten-minute oral exams, again with two meat inspectors and an EHO. We stayed in a hotel the night before the visit to the abattoir for the oral examination. I was flicking through a book I had of pictures of specific diseases. I thought one of the diseases of a chicken had a funny name. It was a picture of a chicken's claws all black: the name of the disease was bumblefoot. Next day at the abattoir I sailed through the first two examiners questions like a breeze. The last examiner was a tough guy who tried the trick of pointing to a fevered carcase asking what this is. I spotted the small tuft of hair on the leg of the carcase, so knew it was a goat not a sheep. So I answered that it was a fevered goat carcase. Many students would not have spotted the tuft of hair and pronounced it's a fevered sheep carcase. Then he pointed to a chicken hanging there with blackened claws. "What is wrong with this chicken?" the examiner asked. "It's a chicken with bumblefoot, sir," I replied. "Yes, that's right," he said. I nearly said, "It is?" After being shown a diseased lamb's liver with liver fluke, I had to recite the life cycle of the parasite that causes liver fluke. Finally I was shown in a jar a tapeworm, which I identified as Taenia saginata, found in cattle, and gave the life cycle of the tapeworm.

After the exams, it was party time and a week or so later I left Manchester to go back home to Lincolnshire. I think Dougie, the leader of the Redditch Fellowship, would like me to have stayed but I knew the Lord wanted me back in Lincolnshire.

Before starting a job in Coningsby as a butcher I went on a tour of Israel with Vincent Matherick, from South Chard Fellowship. I had a great time in Israel and even helped Vincent to baptise two ladies in the River Jordan. When I got back to Heathrow Airport I went to see a lady called Anne who was living in a flat in St George's Hill with a couple of friends. I had met Anne in Chard some years before and she had given me a lift back home to Crawley when I was living there. We had kept in touch by writing mainly spiritual letters to each other. She was very beautiful, and from a middle-class family, quite high up in the nursing profession and I thought quite posh, much above me in life. Notice my inferiority complex coming out there. While staying with Anne it became very evident she wanted a relationship that involved more than writing letters. It was quite a shock that a lady of her standing and beauty would even consider going out with lowly me. A whirlwind romance ensued.

I obtained a job as a butcher in Coningsby, living with my mum in Tattershall. My exam results came through at August time. I had passed every examination with a distinction. I had the Institute of Meat Advanced Certificate, Hollings College Diploma of Meat Technology and, finally, the Royal Institute of Hygiene Certificate of Meat Inspection.

I remember when I opened my letter, my mum saying, "Your dad would have been proud of you, wouldn't he?" Indeed he would have been, having seen me fail all my exams at school. We were told at Hollings that these qualifications were not as high as a degree but certainly HND standard. The Lord had indeed helped me pass every exam: glory and praise to the Lord Jesus. I did try to get a job as a meat inspector, but I didn't have any experience and I couldn't get the experience without first having a job. A bit frustrating at the time but the Lord had other plans lined up which were far better.

Every time I could, I travelled to see Anne living in London, and she would visit me. All was going well, and we even became engaged and were making plans to marry. Anne and her friends in London had been out to North Carolina to a church where they said God was really moving in an amazing way: people were even seeing angels in the services. Sounded good, but I couldn't afford the time or money to go out to North Carolina. One day, I got home to find a letter from Anne. It was a very abrupt, short letter, not like her at all. It said, "Dear Mike, what we thought was right in fact is not, Love, Anne."

I was shocked, confused and dismayed with many questions rushing round in my mind. As soon as I could, I got into my car and went to see Anne at St George's Hill, in Surrey Her friends wouldn't let me see her. A few days later, Anne got on a plane and flew out to the church in Carolina and stayed there six months until her visa ran out. I found out much later that someone at the church in Carolina had heard from God that Anne was not to marry me. This left me bitter at the time and I felt really hurt inside. This experience was feeding my inferiority complex.

I was going to the house groups again in Lincolnshire, taking my guitar, prophesying and sharing the Lord's word. I had made a friend of a young man called Dave Young who used to go to some of the house groups. One day Dave said he was going to visit a fellowship in Kent, and asked if I would like to join him. I said I would love to go with him. I don't remember Dave having a car at the time:

we went in my car.

I was introduced to Alan and Ros Smith and the leaders of the Hempstead Christian Fellowship. I am guessing there were about 60 people in the fellowship at that time. The format of the meetings were Body Ministry, as described earlier; also we had some Bible study given by Clive Arundel at other meetings. I believe we stayed a week in Hempstead.

One night while I was there I had a dream which was given to me by the Holy Spirit. It was as follows. A bus came along, stopped and out of it stepped Anne dressed in a lovely dress, looking beautiful. Right, I thought, I'm going to ask her a load of questions with the intent to condemn her actions. Such questions as: Why hadn't she talked to me after her letter? Why did she just pack her job in as a Sister in a large hospital without notice and just fly off to America? Why didn't she at least talk to me about things? But as I went to speak out my questions and accusations, as I opened my mouth, nothing came out. It was as if I was dumb. Then Anne, looking very peaceful with a nice smile on her face, walked towards a lovely cottage with roses growing all around the doors, like a chocolate box picture. The Holy Spirit then spoke to me and said, "Isn't she wonderful? Isn't she beautiful? She's a lovely lady. She loves me so much. She is a lovely girl." Then she went into the cottage, closed the door and the dream was over. When I awoke in the morning, I knew something had happened in my heart. All the anger and bitterness over Anne had completely gone, and I was free from it all. The joy of the Lord returned, and a closer walk with Him. It was just an amazing experience. Can God set you free from hurts and bondages and heal you while you are fast asleep? Most certainly He can. After spending a wonderful week at Hempstead with David, having great fellowship with the brothers and sisters there, we came back to Lincolnshire. Dave was contemplating moving to Hempstead as he loved the fellowship there. I wondered if that was what God wanted me to do, too. I prayed about it and asked the Lord to open or close the door for a move to Hempstead. As time went by, Dave and I visited Hempstead again. On one visit I heard that there was a new, large store being built, combining Sainsbury's and British Home Stores. It was going to be called Savacentre. To cut a long story short, I applied for a job as a butcher in Savacentre. If the Lord gave me the job, I would move to Hempstead. If the Lord didn't give me the job, I would stay in Lincolnshire. The Lord gave me the job in Savacentre, therefore I moved to Kent. One of the members of Hempstead Christian Fellowship said I could have one of the bedrooms in his house. I cannot recall the exact time I moved, I think it was now 1978. A new chapter was about to unfold in my life that I could never have imagined in a thousand years.

Down South Again

The butchery department at Savacentre employed about eight butchers plus a manager and assistant manager. We worked a 40-hour week with split shifts, meaning one week we started at 7am and finished at 4pm or another week started at 12 noon and finished at 9pm with lunch and tea breaks. We had Sunday and Monday off. The butchery department was on show to the general public because there were large glass windows for people to peer through, watching us prepare the meat. There was the oblong refrigerated well with ladies sat either side weighing and packing the meat ready to go on display in the front counters. The room we worked in was also kept at a cool temperature to keep the meat fresh. It was hard work because we were on our feet all the time and generally rushing around trying to keep all the counters full of product. There was a lot of bending, lifting and walking so I guess it kept me fit and lean. We had some good laughs and discussions while working and I loved the people, all different with interesting backgrounds.

The Hempstead Christian Fellowship was wonderful, full of lovely people who were seeking to walk closer to the Lord Jesus. There was the Sunday meeting held in a room above the Savacentre, then a midweek meeting in what used to be the Hempstead village hall. We also had house group meetings dotted around the Medway towns. Sometimes we gathered in Noreen's house. Noreen was a lady who was a pillar of strength in the fellowship. Her son Simon played the keyboard in our meetings; some of us joined in playing guitars. The meetings were the type I have described before, Body Ministry-type meetings. Lots of lively praise and worship, the gifts of the Holy Spirit and people sharing what God had given them to share. We had specific meetings held for Bible study also. In all our meetings we experienced the wonderful presence of the Lord bringing us peace and joy. Personally I felt really loved and accepted by everyone, a real precious time. There were about ten to fifteen single guys and girls, mostly when I arrived who just kept in their flats or houses at night. So, I used to phone some of them up and get us all together for a meal, a BBQ or to see a film. I remember once we went to the Royal Albert Hall in London to see Andraé Crouch and the Disciples, which was a fun time. I lived with Steve Naven who didn't have a television but was an avid listener of BBC Radio 4. I had never listened to Radio 4 before and found it most strange at first. It amused me that you had PM at 5pm which was a news current affairs programme that lasted an hour full of the news of the day. Then straight afterwards you had the Six O'Clock News where again you listened to most of what you had listened to on the PM programme. I found it bizarre at first then I sort of got into Radio 4, Desert Island Discs with Roy Plomley, Just a Minute, I'm Sorry I Haven't a Clue, Woman's Hour, some comedy programmes and interesting history programmes. Over the years I have enjoyed listening to Radio 4, so a big thankyou to Steve Naven for introducing me to Radio 4.

Steve was quite a good cook, too, introducing me to various dishes. He failed once, though, on the cooking front. He had put the chicken in the oven before going to the Sunday meeting. When we got back the chicken was still in the oven uncooked! He had not put the oven timer on quite right so the oven had not switched itself on. Baked beans on toast for Sunday lunch that day.

We used to have visiting speakers to encourage us at the fellowship. One guy who I felt was very unusual and amusing was Bob Buess. Bob was a six-foot, lean-looking Texan with his high-heeled cowboy boots with fancy decorations on them, his fancy cowboy shirts and Stetson hat. I loved his southern American drawl with his fun sayings like, Aren't you tickled pink with Jay-sus? or I'm a blessing everywhere I go. He had memorised loads of scriptures and his message was one of faith, victory and standing on God's Word.

He taught us that it was a very powerful thing to confess God's Word. He would stand at the front and confess scripture after scripture on any subject. He would tell many stories of impossible situations and how speaking God's Word in faith brought about a change or victory. I loved his message as it tied in with the word Harry Greenwood had given me about slinging the stone, the Word of God, at a giant and cutting its head off with the sword of the Spirit. The truth of God's Word defeats lies that we have believed over the years or lies that the enemy of our souls has spoken to us. Jesus said to His disciples: If you continue in my word (the Word of God) then you shall know the truth and the truth shall make you free. Just after this it says if the Son shall set you free you shall be free indeed. God wants us to be free of any lies or any bondage. Gradually the truth of God's Word was changing me and getting rid of the inferiority complex and other rubbish I had in my life. Harry Greenwood used to say you don't condemn a building while it's being built.

Another visitor we had was Roger Price from Chichester Christian Fellowship. I had met Roger several times since going to John France's wedding to Beryl in 1976. From that time on I had visited CCF quite a few times, going to special events they had put on or going to friends' weddings. Roger was a very gifted talented Bible teacher, he taught us so much of the truth of the Word of God. He had at that time his basic Bible teaching course on cassette tape that was going out all over the place. I have never heard such good Bible teaching as that of Roger Price. When he visited we sometimes had other churches join us and met in a large church building in Rochester. I still love Roger's teaching that is on CD or the web to this day.

Ian Andrews used to come occasionally to minister in a special way healing and miracles. Ian had a very special gift and calling from the Lord in ministering healing and miracles. Many people have received healing and miracles from God under his ministry. For many years he has been teaching the Body of Christ how to move in the gift of healing. He has currently a teaching ministry called Equippers which is online.

I was a bit like a bull in a china shop at this stage of my life, I wasn't very sensitive to people's feelings and needs. I had my faults and idiosyncrasies going on in my life but everyone at the fellowship loved and forgave me, for which I am grateful. I was full of energy, fun and life, being still under 30 years old.

Spiritually I had such a revelation about the covenant blessings in Deuteronomy 28:1-14. It was so clear to me now that our God is a covenant keeping God. In the old covenant if the Children of Israel hearkened unto the voice of the Lord their God and obeyed His Commandments all these blessings listed in Deuteronomy 28:1-14 was theirs. If they turned away from the Lord then curses followed as listed from verses 15 to 68. However, the new covenant that is through Christ's sacrifice on the cross means as believers and followers of Jesus Christ we can have the blessings listed 1-14 and not have the curses because, according to Galatians 3:13, Christ has redeemed us from the curse of the law by becoming a curse for us, for it is written: "Cursed is everyone who is hung on a pole (or tree)." I prayed out loud confessing the covenant blessings, claiming them for my life by faith, just like Bob Buess taught us to do. I praised the Lord that I had been bought out from the curses of the Lord by the blood of Christ, I have been redeemed. When I pray for people nowadays I still pray the covenant blessings 1-14 in Deuteronomy. I am amazed how many believers don't know about the covenant blessings. This revelation also tied in with the prophecy from Harry Greenwood for in the story of David and Goliath David states, "Who are these uncircumcised Philistines?" In other words David was saying we have a covenant with our God that says any enemy that rises up against you one way will flee before you in seven directions. The Philistines didn't have a covenant with God. David knew he was in covenant relationship with his mighty God and had faith he could defeat this giant Goliath.

Savacentre was thriving: we had our work cut out keeping the meat counters full of product. The management asked us to work overtime because they were short of staff. I threw myself into helping out by working double shifts, meaning starting at 7am and leaving at 9pm. Financially this meant time and half pay for 40 hours a week then flat pay the other 40 hours. After working 80 hours a week for two or three months it began to wear me out, even with all my energy. I asked my house group to pray as I sought a career move, I wanted to use my qualifications and wanted to claim the covenant blessing for a career. I could see the meat trade was going to change and it wouldn't be long before all the meat products would be arriving already packaged from a central depot. It was just obvious that the way we were operating at Savacentre and other superstores was too labour-intensive and inefficient. This has proven to be the case: nowadays most large supermarkets have just one or two qualified butchers in their employ.

One day one of the butchers at Savacentre told me of a vacancy being advertised in the Meat Trades Journal for an area representative for Hobart Manufacturing Co Limited. I replied, "What's an area representative do, then?" "Oh it's easy, you just go round seeing companies representing your company." "Oh ok," I said. I obtained the advertisement and applied for the job not knowing really what I was applying for. About a week or so later I had a letter inviting me to attend an interview at the Crawley branch of Hobart. On the day of the interview I put on the only suit I had and polished up my shoes and off I went. I was met by a gentleman called Bill Henwood who looked a tad like Colonel Sanders of Kentucky Fried Chicken fame. I entered his office and he explained what Hobart were looking for and what the job entailed. He asked me several questions. Then explained I would be getting a company car then have a basic salary plus commission. All this sounded completely foreign to me, a basic salary, commission? Then Bill asked me if I would like a cup of tea. Oh, yes please, I replied. He went out and I was left pondering what to do. Then as clear as a bell I heard the Lord say to me four words.

I will prosper you. When Bill came back with a cup of tea he asked me would I like to go to the next stage of interviews. Yes please, I replied. Two weeks later, I had another interview with two gentlemen, one was from the Hobart head office in London. I got on very well with them both and at the end of the interview they offered me the job as area representative for their meat-processing equipment covering London. Two weeks of training followed in one of Hobart's offices in London whereupon I was given a Ford Estate car only a year old. I had tons of energy and lots of enthusiasm, willing to learn all they threw at me. There was a gentleman called Terry Smith at Head Office who was the product manager for meat-processing equipment for Hobart. He took me under his wing. He could see my potential and advised me what books to buy on the basics of selling. I duly bought all the books and devoured them and tried out the techniques as I went out cold-calling on every business that was processing meat. I was still living in Gillingham with Steve Naven and travelling into London daily in my car. I found out driving in London was hard work by the end of the week I was tired out as I was averaging about 90 calls a week. I found out later it's not the number of calls you make it's the quality of the calls you make. I was naïve about selling: I had lots to learn about my new profession. With help from others I managed to make some sales. I loved meeting new people and talking about my products, I found it really good fun, better than standing behind a butcher's block all day long! Life at Hempstead Christian Fellowship was great, I had made some new friends, and I loved the meetings and the Bible studies.

I was still praying the verses in Deuteronomy 28:1-14. The Lord had changed my career and said He would prosper me, so I felt that the Lord had fulfilled part of His covenant. Another part of the covenant blessing stated that the Lord would bless the fruit of your womb. I had prayed Lord, I haven't got a womb, please provide a womb. In other words Lord, please provide a wife for me.

I used to visit Chichester Christian Fellowship quite often at this time, especially if Roger Price was teaching at one of the conferences they put on. One of the young ladies called Jacqui Worthly, in the fellowship in Hempstead, had moved to live in Chichester. Jacqui was living in a house called

Clydesdale in Chichester with a young, married couple called Ian and Juliet Ryall. One weekend as I was visiting Chichester I thought I would go and see Jacqui to see how she was getting on in her new abode. She answered the door at Clydesdale and showed me into the sitting room where she had been reading. In the corner of the room sat a young lady doing some artwork: she had a large, curly hairstyle, quite unusual, I thought.

Jacqui said, "This is Jenny." I smiled and said hello and we all had a cup of tea and a chat together about life in Chichester. Jenny, I found out later, was illustrating Roger Price's first book called *In the Beginning*. That was my first meeting with Jenny New and much, much later it became very significant that it was Jacqui who had introduced us to each other. Whenever I visited Chichester Christian Fellowship I used to see Jenny in the meetings, usually dancing before the Lord. (We used to praise the Lord with dancing as well as singing in our meetings.) On one visit to Chichester Ian and Juliet invited me to have tea with them at Clydesdale House. When I arrived there were quite a number of people all chatting away. I had a chat with Jenny and thought she was a very nice lady. Little did I know that the Lord spoke to her at this time together and He told her that I was going to be her husband! She was so shocked apparently that she rushed upstairs to the loo to pray. I had no idea that the Lord had spoken to Jenny about me whatsoever. Some months later, I did ask Jenny out to dinner and after that we started going out with each other: I had fallen in love with the girl with curly hair. After a few months going out with Jenny I asked her to marry me, and she said yes. By this time Jenny had moved with Ian and Juliet to live in a house called South Bank in Chichester near the canal. One day Jenny said she wanted to take me down the canal to meet the ducks. Apparently one day when Jenny had been walking down the canal she had come across three ducks sitting on the bank. She had said out loud to the ducks that God had said to her He was going to provide a husband for her. When I have found my future husband, she said, I will bring him here to show you him, hence I was taken down the canal to meet the ducks. For a bit of fun I got down on one knee in front of the ducks and proposed to Jenny. I thought later on, Ok, Jenny has shown the ducks her future husband. I will take Jenny to show her to my friends Malcolm and Kitty Muggeridge. I picked Jenny up and told her we were going for a surprise trip to East Sussex. Halfway there I told her who we were going to see. Malcolm and Kitty welcomed Jenny with open arms and gave us both a lovely time having tea, sandwiches and home-made cakes. What a real delight it was. I loved Malcolm and Kitty: they were both so warm and kind to us both.

After talking and praying about where to live, London, Gillingham or Chichester, it was obvious it was Chichester. I found a job working for a company in Portsmouth selling meat-processing equipment and I moved to live in Chichester with a couple in the fellowship there. I had met Jenny's mum and dad who lived in Waterlooville, the wedding date had been arranged for the 8th of August 1981, or abbreviated 8th of 8th 1981, 8/8/81. To me it was significant as 8 is the number in the Bible that means resurrection life. Each letter has a numerical value in Greek, the numerical value of the letters in the name "Jesus" in Greek add up to 888. Jesus equals resurrection, resurrection, resurrection. He even said, "I am the resurrection and the life". Therefore I believed 8/8/81 was saying: Make Jesus (888) 1st (first) in your marriage and you will be ok. Which we both endeavoured to do. Our wedding was full of joy and love. We got married in the Baptist church in Bognor Regis. John France was my best man, Roger Price took the marriage ceremony, Ian and Juliet sang, as did Chris, Clive Dave and Annie from Hempstead Christian Fellowship. The reception was in a marquee on a big lawn of a house near Fontwell Park Racecourse. Some of the people from Chichester Fellowship did a marvellous job doing the catering for us. We went off on our honeymoon to Tenby in South Wales.

We had managed to get a mortgage for a mid-terraced house in Charles Avenue for only £22,000: today that only buys a new car. When we got back we were overwhelmed with all the wedding gifts stacked up in the lounge diner. We felt really blessed by God.

Jenny was teaching a reception class at Mill Rythe Infant School on Hayling Island which she really enjoyed. I, on the other hand, was finding it hard to get sales for the new company in Portsmouth. At that time butchers' shops were closing down so the market was flooded with second-hand meat-processing equipment. The owner called me into his office one Friday afternoon and gave me a week's notice to quit. It was quite a blow at the time. I got friends to pray about this situation and I got peace that everything was going to be alright. I finished with the company on the Friday afternoon. Then that night I had a phone call from a cheery guy called Keith McDermott from Hobart. He introduced himself and said he had heard that I was looking for a job. I can only think it must have been Terry Smith at Hobart's head office in London who had informed Keith. Keith invited me to go and see him on Monday morning. We instantly got on with each other like a house on fire. He gave me the position of area sales representative for West Sussex selling catering equipment. This was a new adventure, a complete change of product and market I had no idea about whatsoever. Was I going to succeed? was the question.

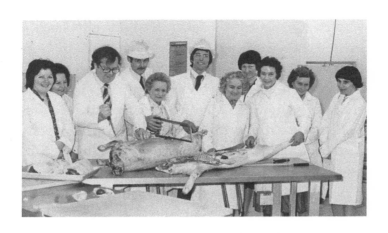

High Flying And Family

The Hobart regional office for the South East was based at that time in Crawley, and this is where I had my initial interview with Bill Henwood. It was here that I turned up one Monday morning to commence my training in catering equipment and learn about the marketplace I would be selling into. The product range was vastly different to what I had been used to in the meat trade. I was keen to learn all about this new range of equipment: I still had tons of energy and enthusiasm. If I do anything in life I do it with all my heart with everything I have, full on. I don't like doing things half measure.

After two weeks of intensive training I was let out on the road in my new car, price book and catalogue. I was told I could go anywhere in West Sussex and half of East Sussex into any establishment where they prepared, cooked and sold food. This included restaurants, hotels, in-flight catering at Gatwick Airport, colleges, schools, bakeries, food production kitchens. Suddenly I was talking to totally different kinds of people. My saving grace was that everybody in the catering industry knew Hobart through the very good marketing and the very well established brand name Hobart. Hobart equipment had a reputation for being high-quality, reliable equipment with excellent service and spare parts back-up. I used to make my first calls around eight o'clock in the morning to bakers as they were finishing their night shifts, then cold-call restaurants, café, hotels. In the afternoon I visited hospital catering managers. Making appointments is a skill I had to learn, as the receptionist's job is to keep away from their bosses any time-wasters.

Gatwick Airport was in my area where there is an enormous amount of in-flight catering. A whole new world opened up seeing behind the scenes how the meals for airlines were produced and supplied to the aircraft. Any delay in getting the trolleys of meals to the aircraft could attract large financial penalties for delaying the plane from taking off. Hobart supplied large, tunnel-type warewashers to enable a quick turnaround of trolleys and trays. These machines were something like 30-40 feet long with prewash, wash, final rinse of 82 degrees centigrade, and finally a warm-air dryer. If I found a company interested in replacing such a machine I had a technical guy to back me up who also did drawings if needed. We would visit the site to measure up and make sure all the correct services were available. Just one of these machines would cost around £35,000 in 1982.

I loved meeting different kinds of people. However, I still struggled with an inferiority complex, so I found it hard meeting directors of large companies, hotel head chefs, catering managers of hospitals, universities, colleges etc. One day I was out with Keith McDermott for the day and my nervousness about going to the next call to visit a director of a large company was showing. He said, "Mike, the more you do it, the easier it will become. Remember, you are the expert on the Hobart product range, they are just people in the end." After a few months, my confidence was growing and the inferiority complex was gradually subsiding bit by bit. I know God was working in my life to set me free from my inferiority complex. Jesus said, "You shall know the truth and the truth shall make you free." I had a sales target to reach but the great thing was that I was credited for any Hobart equipment that ended up on my patch. I used to pray for orders to come in and they did. I was still learning different sales techniques from books, videos and my colleagues in the company. I knew the Lord was with me and I continued to claim His promises in the Word of God, the Bible.

In 1983 Hobart arranged for about twenty of us to go to Offenburg, Germany, to visit their factory and school of training. We had two weeks intensive training starting at 8am and finishing at 5.30pm. We went through all the product range as well as actually seeing the machines being made. We stayed in the same hotel, therefore in the evenings we all went out for meals and fun. On the middle Saturday and Sunday we visited a small town where the streets were full of cuckoo clocks of every description. Also we visited Baden-Baden where they have a famous casino. We went to the Black Forest walking, as do the Germans, and stopped off for the evening meal in a low, chalet-style building. They found out I played the guitar and duly produced one. I entertained them with Beatles songs and campfire songs from my Boy Scout days. It was a good, fun evening full of food, laughter and wine.

Jenny had longed to have children: at this time she was pregnant with our first child. When I got back from Germany Jenny greeted me at Bognor railway station. I remember her being large with child – it was the beginning of September. I remember feeling overwhelming love for Jenny as she sometimes struggled to cope with pregnancy. The time came one night that Jenny's waters broke and an ambulance was called to take her to St Richard's Hospital in Chichester. I duly followed, thinking I would be out within a couple of hours. I didn't know anything about childbirth whatsoever. Hours passed as the process of delivering the baby went on... and on... and on. Nineteen hours after we arrived, the doctors and nurses began rushing about. I was put into a side room. The baby had turned round the wrong way and didn't want to come out the normal way, and it was becoming stressed. Jenny was rushed into the operating theatre and given a Caesarean section birth. I had no idea what this meant but half an hour later I was given a bundle of cloth with a baby boy in it. Jenny was wheeled in on a bed, shaking as she came out of the anaesthetic. I nearly dropped the baby as I wondered why Jenny was shaking. The nurse said that's normal after an operation like she has just had. After a while, I was kneeling besides the bed congratulating her, saying, Well done, we have a wonderful baby boy. We were both overwhelmed with such great joy, love and peace. We named our son Peter John, Peter meaning rock and John meaning love. We had loads of visitors come to see our new baby boy: it was a very special, precious time for both of us.

After a couple of weeks in hospital Jenny came out of hospital to our mid-terraced house in Chichester. We were family. In the Bible the parents of the baby called their children names which described their characters. They were experts at recognising what the child was going to be like as they grew up. I am thinking of Jacob when being born, grabbing Esau's ankle. Jacob means supplanter or schemer, which he turned out to be, cheating his brother out of his birthright. Later on, Jacob wrestled with an angel clinging onto him, wanting to know his name and wanting a blessing. The angel touched his thigh leaving him with a limp, but also a change of name from Jacob to Israel, which means struggle with God.

Peter has turned out to be a great guy. He hasn't gone the usual route in life of school college/ university or apprenticeship. When he left school, he started breakdancing and made a career out of it. I was feeling frustrated with him, asking why he didn't train to be a plumber or an electrician. He made a career out of breakdancing, working on the same stage as famous singers, making videos, making adverts for Adidas, for example. He also worked for Duggie Dug Dug, a guy who does Christian Praise parties for churches. I used to say he goes to church more than me. When he was 30 years old he changed tack completely. He started making architectural models, eventually getting into 3D printing working for Ecco Shoes in Amsterdam on product development. He met and fell in love with a lady called Lena who lives in Munich. He left Ecco in Amsterdam and at the moment he is involved in virtual reality drawing for a large company. He had a word given him when he was dedicated, "The Blessing of the Lord makes one rich and adds no sorrow with it." That word has come to pass in his life to the letter. He presently works for this large company in Munich, commanding a large income. He was given another word by someone when he was dedicated that he would be a prophet to the nation. I am waiting for that word to be fulfilled.

As time went by we had two more wonderful children, Katie Elizabeth and Jack William. Katie's birth was a struggle, but she arrived here in the end. That's just like Katie has been: she has had her struggles in life but she has turned out to be a wonderful young lady. Katie did foundation art and then went to university and obtained a degree in fine art. She is pursuing a career in art at the same time as working for the county council to pay her way in life, until she gets discovered as an artist. Katie has had several exhibitions in Chichester. She, too, had words from the Lord, some which have come to pass and some which are yet to come to pass. Words about bitter waters becoming sweet, this has given her compassion for those who struggle in life. Katie is a very kind, lovely lady indeed.

When Jack was born it was very quick and easy. When he was born it was like he was announcing, "Here I am. What's next?" Jack has turned out to be a great man, a gentle giant. He, too, was given words from the Lord when he was dedicated, such as he would be a worshipper. This has come to pass in that he learnt to play the drums and often plays the drums in church.

I have come to realise just recently our family is very important to God, for it is God who in the beginning created the heavens and the earth, then Adam and Eve so that He could have a family. God had the angels and all of Heaven but he didn't have anyone who had free will to worship Him or reject Him. Free will is important to God and he won't force you to do anything. He will ask you or show you quite clearly what He would like you to do, but He will never force anyone to do anything. God is love. It is God who invented the marriage of a man and a woman to populate the earth and provide a secure, loving family unit in which children may grow. Today, the family unit is under attack from the enemy of our souls, and society, in general.

I believe there is an order of priority for followers of Christ to adhere to, namely God first, family second, Church third, and world next. I am aware of scriptures that one could quote to the contrary but in life, in general, I believe we have to look after family, then our brothers and sisters in Christ. In the Gospel of John, Jesus is suffering on the cross in pain and agony. He looks down and sees his mother Mary and the disciple, John, and says to her, "Woman, here is your son," then He says to John, "Here is your mother," and from that hour he took her into his home. Then if you read the letters that John wrote in the New Testament carefully, you can see the whole concept of putting God first, then family, and the Church being family, and how we are to love and care for one another as brothers and sisters.

The Apostle Paul says we are to be tender-hearted towards one another, forgiving one another even as Christ forgave us. When I was visiting my brother-in-law in Abu Dhabi we watched a film at The Club, called *The Railway Man*, all about how the Japanese tortured soldiers in the war when they were building a railway. After the war had ended, the soldier had come to a place where he forgave his torturer and they became best friends. What a great example of forgiveness that is. I am certain there are many more such stories to be told.

I am so grateful to the Lord for giving me such a wonderful family in the natural, my physical blood family and the great wider family of God, my spiritual family. If you are at this moment without a blood natural family, be of good cheer because you have the family of God to enjoy.

When we were first married, Jenny and I were in the Chichester Christian Fellowship. We felt we were in the best Christian fellowship in the world – a true family who loved one another. We had great meetings where the Holy Spirit moved among us, speaking to us through the words that were shared or the gifts of the Holy Spirit such as prophecy, tongues and interpretation of tongues, visions, words of knowledge and wisdom. If anyone was sick, we would pray for them to be healed. We also had a very gifted Bible teacher in Roger Price. We all loved Roger and his teaching was second to none. We loved our weekly house groups and social times we had together. I think there were about four hundred of us all together.

We had to divide into two congregations at one point, because we were breaking fire regulations in the hall in Chichester that we hired. It was a difficult decision but it had to be done. We had one congregation which met in Chichester, and another one which met in Bognor Regis.

All was going really well, then we had some really bad news announced one evening in 1985. Roger announced he had been diagnosed with cancer of the throat. It was devastating news to the fellowship but really devastating news for Roger's wife Ros and the young children David and Karen. We all rallied round Roger and his family supporting them the best we knew how. We set ourselves to fast and pray for Roger's healing. We alerted everyone who knew and loved Roger in this country and abroad. It was a very testing and difficult time for all of us. People had words such as you shall live and not die. The last thing anyone wanted was for Roger to die. Alas, in January 1986, our dear brother died. Why didn't God heal Roger? It was a real blow to our faith in God and our understanding of God's Word, and our theology. It was a terrific loss to the Chichester Christian Fellowship (CCF) and the wider Body of Christ. Roger had been visiting many fellowships in the UK and was becoming well known in other parts of the world. His Bible studies were being recorded and sent out on cassette tapes, and his talks are still going out from CCF Tapes at Bognor Regis to this day, plus there are his Bible studies on the web.

With Roger now gone who would lead the CCF?

We had several Elders but it was to be John France, one of the Elders who had been alongside Roger for many years, who took on the main role of leadership, along with the other elders in support. John was and still is a very good teacher of the Word of God, but one has to say he has a different style to Roger Price altogether. Things didn't change all at once, but, over the years, numbers went down as people moved away to different parts of the world or joined other Church fellowships nearby. The Bognor Regis side of CCF eventually became known as the Kingsgate Church. There was no pianist in the Chichester side of the fellowship. My good friend Juliet Ryall came to our house one day and asked if I would like to join her and a young man called John Mason to lead the praise and worship. I had been playing guitar for years in home groups, so knew a lot of the songs. The three of us had different styles, Juliet was folky, John was classically trained and I was rocky. We blended quite well together, we prayed and practised on a Wednesday evening and had a rough plan of what songs to sing on Sunday.

Lots of things occurred in the Chichester side of CCF, some very painful times as one half of the congregation wanted to completely separate from the Bognor Regis side of CCF. We had a meeting and a vote and the side that wanted to separate from Bognor left and joined other churches in Chichester over time. Sadly some people stopped going anywhere for a while. We had made friends with a couple who had joined the fellowship and we had become very close. They invited us to go with them to Stoneleigh Conference near Coventry one year. Stoneleigh Conference was run by New Frontiers International (NFI) based in Brighton but with churches all over the UK. They hired the Stoneleigh Showground and twenty thousand plus people attended over two separate weeks. The main leader of NFI was Terry Virgo who invited internationally well-known Christian speakers to the event. The praise and worship music was loud and great, I loved the meetings. This was now 1995/6 and there was the Toronto Blessing going on at this time. People were mightily touched by the Holy Spirit in various ways such as being filled with great amounts of joy and laughter. Jenny and I attended Stoneleigh a few years running.

The close friends we had had suddenly turned against Jenny and me, and they rejected us. Rejection is a very painful thing to live with, it caused us both literal pains in our hearts and bodies. I tried to sort things out by writing letters but things went from bad to worse. I learnt a lot through all this deep valley of rejection. It was a dark time for us both. Now if anyone is in a similar situation to this, I would say the best thing to do is forgive, let go and do nothing, and let God move. This is more easily said than done. I felt really ashamed of my reactions during this time of rejection, and, sadly, I left CCF and joined a new fellowship called Chichester Community Church (CCC) that had just been started by a lady called Pam Gathercole and her friend Julie Bowling. Pam was under the oversight of the leaders of a church in Horsham called Kingdom Faith: it was headed up by Colin Urquhart.

Almost straight away I was asked to lead the praise and worship with my guitar along with a guy called Peter, who played guitar also. A lady called Annette joined Peter and me: she kept me in key and in tune, and she has a wonderful singing voice. I used to meet with Peter on a weeknight to practise songs and get a plan together for Sunday. We had some wonderful times together worshipping the Lord and entering His presence. Peter had only just lost his wife at such a young age and found these times together strengthening. I had at that time no idea whatsoever what great a time of grief that Peter was going through. He did a magnificent job taking care of his two young children. Jenny and our children joined CCC, and gradually the pains caused by rejection began to be healed but it took a long time.

After a few years Pam stepped down from leading CCC and I felt it was time for me to move on. I began to go to Yapton Free Church where a guy called Hugo was the main leader. Jenny didn't feel like going all the way to Yapton; for a while, she went nowhere in particular. I enjoyed meeting with the fellowship in

Yapton. One day Jenny heard about a New Frontiers church starting up in Chichester area. I had previously asked the Lord to start an NFI church up locally and promised if He started one up I would join it. The first meeting we went to was held in Oving Village Hall, a man called Steve Petch was preaching and his wife Jo was leading worship. We both felt very at home almost immediately: I will tell you in a later chapter what happened next.

The Chichester side of CCF eventually became less and less. Ian, Juliet's husband, was asked to be pastoral elder in the fellowship in Midhurst, which he did for three years, before eventually they decided to move to Spain.

We all treasure in our hearts the wonderful times we had together with one another in CCF, and we who are still in touch with one another are still family, and we still love one another. I think it is fair to say that we have not found anything quite like what we had in CCF. Quite a few of our brothers and sisters have joined Roger in Heaven. One day we will all join them and have a great party, I am sure. How wonderful it is that this life on earth is not the real deal: we have the best yet to come in eternity. No wonder the apostle Paul urges us to rejoice in the Lord always and again I say, Rejoice! Also he wrote that our present suffering is not worthy to be compared to the glory that shall be revealed in us.

Selling

As stated earlier, Deuteronomy 28:1-14 sets out the covenant blessing that God promises Israel, if they will listen to Him and walk in His ways. If Israel didn't listen to God's voice and obey His Commandments, then there is listed a number of curses, the curse of the law. This was under the Old Covenant. We read in Galatians 3:13 that "Christ has redeemed us from the curse of the law, for as it is written cursed is he who hangs on the tree." We read in Hebrews, in great detail, how the new covenant is a better covenant by far than the old one. Jesus Christ's death on the cross, and His resurrection, brought in this new and better covenant.

In my new job with Hobart, I often prayed for the Lord to bless the work of my hands and make me the head and not the tail. The key I found to receiving these blessings in business was to listen to the Lord's voice and obey. Jesus said, "My sheep hear my voice." I claim by faith daily that I am one of his sheep, so I can hear His voice. I would like to share with you now a few examples of me hearing the Lord speaking to me, and the blessing that followed in my career in selling.

HASLAR

The sales books teach you to **"Plan your Work, Work your Plan"** and again **"If you aim at nothing you're bound to hit it"**, and "If **you don't know where you are going it doesn't matter which bus you catch"**. In general, I followed this advice of planning and goal setting. I loved Zig Ziglar's books and tapes on this subject. He was a very inspirational speaker. There were exceptions to this advice, though. One day, I had planned to visit the Horsham area as I had an appointment with a lady who was in charge of procurement in a private Japanese school, called Rikkyo School, and then I was going to do cold-calling around Horsham restaurants and hotels.

I came out of my appointment at the school at about 10 o'clock, and I prayed and asked the Lord where I should go next. I was expecting Him to say a restaurant or hotel in Horsham or nearby. Instead I just heard one word **"HASLAR"** as clear as a bell. Hearing the voice of God is like having a transistor radio on with no control on the volume. Sometimes it's very clear and loud, other times it's very faint and you have to decide whether it's really God speaking or your own imagination or thought life. This particular time was very clear. Haslar was the short name of a customer Hobart had called the Royal Naval Hospital Haslar, in Gosport. I now had to decide what to do. Should I ignore the Lord's voice as ludicrous, as Gosport was over two hours' drive away? We were taught time behind a steering wheel is dead time: we needed to be in front of the buyers or decision-makers to make best use of our time. I decided to step out in faith and go to Haslar in Gosport.

As I was driving along, I phoned the chief engineer, Gary, to tell him I was calling in to see him. (Hands-free phone of course.) He said, "Oh good. The Facility Manager wants to see you." Oh dear, I thought, maybe it's about the problems with the ovens I sold them last month. I said I would be there about midday. On checking through security and arriving onsite I met up with Gary and the Facility Manager in the staff restaurant. "Right," they said, "we want to go through your catalogue and choose new equipment for the galley and wards." We duly went through my catalogue choosing equipment for the kitchen and dishwashers for the wards. Then I was shown to a private office with a large desk and telephone and asked to make sure my company could deliver and invoice the chosen equipment by the 31st of March. After checking we could fulfil the required delivery and invoice dates I had to fill in their procurement document with product codes and prices. In short I came out with an order for £85,000. This was well over my target for March in one order. **Thank you, Lord.**

SPREAD EAGLE

One day I thought I would spend a day in Worthing, calling on my existing customers and cold-calling for new business. Most sales people hate cold-calling as it's tough being rejected call after call. I quite enjoyed cold-calling as you never knew what was round the corner, and it's nice meeting new people. It's a question of attitude. I liked the acronym ACE which means Attitude, Confidence, Enthusiasm.

Attitude: To be a good salesperson you have to have a positive attitude to life and the job. You have to be a half-full glass person, not a half-empty glass person. If you have the wrong negative attitude you won't sell much.

Confidence: You need to be a confident person and confident in the product you are selling. You are helping people to choose the best product for their business. The product that will save time and money long-term and give them less downtime ease of use.

Enthusiasm: To be a good salesperson you need to be enthusiastic and have enthusiasm about what you are doing and about the product you are selling.

I believe I had been blessed with all of the above.

As I was driving along the A27 to Worthing from Chichester I came to the Arundel roundabout. I felt the Lord tell me to turn right towards Ford. As I drove towards Ford I asked the Lord where I was going. He said, "Bailiffscourt Hotel." "What?" I thought, "They are bankrupt and under liquidation."

A family called Lamb had failed to make a success of this nice hotel. The hotel had been built to look like an old, 17th-century, oldy-worldly-type building on the outside. Inside, there were no visible signs of heating radiators as these were hidden within the walls. Little did I know the hotel had been bought and taken over by some new people, the Goodmans. I called in at the reception desk and asked for the head chef or catering manager. I introduced myself and my company to the manager who said, "Actually, we are looking for a new glasswasher out the back." I duly measured, surveyed for correct services and quoted the machine. A few days later they ordered the machine and it was installed. I called in to demonstrate to the staff how to use the machine correctly. I left some leaflets and card. A few weeks later the lady owner of Bailiffscourt Hotel, Mrs Goodman, rang me up and asked if I would meet her at The Spread Eagle Hotel in Midhurst. I had been trying to get into this prestigious hotel for ages with no success. I didn't know that Mrs Goodman owned The Spread Eagle and another high-market hotel at Cuckfield, called Ockenden Manor. Mrs Goodman was upgrading the kitchen at The Spread Eagle. After several meetings and surveys, I was given an order for £65,000. **Glory to God!**

HASLAR AGAIN

I had kept in touch with all my contacts at Royal Naval Hospital Haslar, in Gosport, even though there was rumours of the hospital closing down. They were having a major refurb of the kitchen and wanted a special type of dishwasher. The machine they wanted was a tunnel conveyor-type machine called a Flight machine (developed for the in-flight catering trade) which wasn't too unusual. What was unusual was that they wanted a final rinse of 80 degrees centigrade on the plates. This was to give thermal disinfection, which was becoming more popular in wards as a small, front-loading type of dishwasher, but not in tunnel machines. I quoted this specialised type of machine which priced up at £52,000. I lost the order to a competitor whose price was £30,000. I felt the Lord say, **"Don't give up."**

I spoke to my technical advisor at head office. He said to ask the facility engineers at the hospital how the competitor's machine was going to achieve 80 °C on the plates. I did this and their answer came back saying they would turn the elements up higher in the wash tanks. The technical advisor said that it would burn the elements out and would not rinse with fresh, clean water at 80 °C on the plates from a boiler as per the DHSS guidelines. The machine I had quoted had a 60-gallon boiler in it with eight sets of rinse arms giving 80C on the plates. The facility manager cancelled the order with the competitors and gave it to me. **Thank you, Lord.**

HEAD NOT THE TAIL

At the beginning of one year, I prayed and claimed the verse in Deuteronomy 28:13 about the Lord making you the head and not the tail above and not beneath. I prayed, "Lord, please, make me the winner of the Chairman's Cup this year." The Chairman's Cup was given each year to the top salesman in the company. There were 50 salesmen/women to compete against, so it was not easy to achieve. As the year went on, the sales I had been working on suddenly came live and orders came flooding in from all over the place. At the regional sales meeting one salesman said, "Hello, Mike's been getting his prayer mat out again!" Another salesman said, "Can I borrow it?" I said, "No, you have to get your own!"

That year I won the Chairman's Cup, and it was presented with a nice cheque at the winners' dinner in London. At the regional Christmas party held at Bristol in January there was a new young salesman called David, who had only just joined Hobart. He said to his wife pointing at me, "This is Mike Davis. He won the Chairman's Cup last year." He was sitting on a sofa and I was standing up with my wife Jenny. I pointed to him and prophesied to him that this year he would win the Chairman's Cup. As the new sales year progressed, it came to November and it was obvious David was going to be top salesman. He rang me up telling me that what I said had come to pass. I told him it was the Lord who had made him a winner to fulfil His word. He was presented the Chairman's Cup at the winners' dinner held at the Grosvenor House Hotel in London. That year the theme of the night was called a night of a thousand stars. The true star is Jesus, one of the names He is called is The **Bright and Morning Star**.

I was always in the top fifteen salesmen in the company charts. I put it all down to the covenant blessing in Deuteronomy 28.

I left Hobart to join a small company in Portsmouth called BFES who had promised more money, better car etc. After six or seven months, the sales didn't come in and they couldn't afford to keep me on. The very day I was given this news, I had a visit from one of their companies suppliers, a sales manager called Nick, who worked for Winterhalter. Winterhalter is a German company manufacturing all kinds of top-end warewashing machines. They had just bought a company called Classic Ware Washing based in Stafford who manufactured machines at the lower end of the market. They were looking for a new salesman to cover the South East. Nick had a word with the Managing Director David Smithson and, after an interview, I was employed. I have never been without a job since leaving school at fifteen. This new sales job was different to what I had been used to. Classic supplied companies with warewashing and ice-makers, who then sold to end-users, usually a pub or restaurant. My role was to support the distributors and make sure they knew the latest about our machines, do site surveys and basically keep them happy.

I covered the South East, London, Norfolk and Suffolk. It was quite a large area which meant staying away in hotels and a lot of driving. I continued to claim the covenant blessings and asked the Lord to bring in the sales. The Lord, ever faithful, brought in the sales, making me a great success. I enjoyed entertaining the company's customers by taking them to rugby matches or Lord's Cricket Ground, all the meals out. After a year or so, they asked me to cover the South West which I tried to do, but living in Chichester it took me four hours to reach, say, Barnstable. I got really tired doing all the driving, and I didn't want to move house. Then the German head office said they wanted to cut the number of salesman working for Classic. If one of us volunteered to leave they would pay us severance money. I decided to leave and take the money.

I joined one of my distributors in Kent for a while, working as their salesman. A job came to my attention at a small company called DC, based in Somerset. I went for an interview in Wells and, a few days later, I was offered a position as Business Development Manager for the South East. I worked for DC for the next few years until I retired in 2014. When I started working for DC, the South East area was bringing in £350,000 a year. When I left the company, the sales were increased to over £1.3m. Another great success. I worked part-time for a small company in Portsmouth for a while, then finally hung up my order book.

I really enjoyed my successful career in sales. Overall it was such fun, and it was great meeting so many different kinds of people. I am forever grateful to the Lord for blessing my working life, ultimately working for Him. The Bible says, "Work as unto the Lord, not as unto man as man a pleaser… whatsoever you do in word or deed do all in the Name of Jesus." Thank you, Lord, for all you have done. Glory to Jesus. Amen.

Jenny

I want to tell you about the lady who became my
wife, lover and best ever friend. Jenny was born in
September 1955 in Portsmouth, England, to her parents
Harry and Betty New. Betty was a schoolteacher and
Harry started his career in Portsmouth Dockyard in
the stores. He worked his way up to be the Principal
Foreman to the Naval Stores. Jenny had an older
brother called Richard. They lived in a house in
Waterlooville just outside Portsmouth. Not long after
Jenny was born Harry had a posting to Sri Lanka
(Ceylon). Betty and the children sailed out to be with
Harry and set up home in Trincomalee Naval Base.
Because Harry had risen to a high position in naval
stores, the family had a nanny for the children and a
housekeeper to clean the house and cook the meals.
What luxury. We have pictures of Jenny's nanny
and the lovely house that the Navy provided. In the
summer, most families spent their holidays away in
the mountains because it was cooler there.

After a short time back in England, the family
went to Malta where Jenny and Richard continued

their education. Again, the family had a servant to cook, wash and clean, and even a gardener. This left a lot of time for Harry and Betty to play tennis, socialise and go to the beaches in Malta. When the posting in Malta ended, the family moved back into the house in Waterlooville. Both Richard and Jenny completed their education at local schools. Jenny was very artistic, she had a great talent to draw and paint. She wanted to go to art school but her parents insisted she was to be a qualified as a teacher. They felt the artistic route was not a secure career choice to take. At the time the schools were crying out for new teachers. Jenny went to Bishop Otter College (1972/73 I think), because, at that time, the college was focused on training teachers, and was not a university, as it is now. She lived in the halls of residence where she made good friends with Helen and Karen who were Christians. There came a point that Jenny heard about Jesus coming back again. Helen and Karen hadn't told Jenny about this fact and she was upset that they hadn't told her. Helen told her the gospel story but she wanted to find out if it was really true.

One day as she sat in her room she spoke out into thin air, "Jesus, if you are alive, and what I have been hearing is true, please show me." At that point, the sun shone into the room casting a shadow of a cross and, as well as that, there came a wonderful presence of God. Jenny gave her heart and life to Christ that day and was born again. She was changed forever.

Helen and Karen were going to Chichester Christian Fellowship (CCF) and so Jenny joined them. CCF became Jenny's second family, they loved her and took her into their hearts and lives. Soon she was baptised in water and was prayed for the baptism of the Holy Spirit and she began to speak in tongues just like they did in Acts chapter 2. This experience with God changed Jenny and she committed her life to serve the Lord in any way she could, and loved being in the fellowship. She wrote a song at that time telling how she felt.

> Nobody but you Lord, Nobody but You
> No man will I follow, Nobody but You
> You're my life, My hope, My confidence
> Now you're all I need
> Knowing the Love of Jesus
> It's only You I see

Jenny finished her three-year training course and qualified as a teacher. She decided to stay in Chichester, living with various people in the fellowship. She obtained a job in Farnham first of all then after a few years ended up teaching in Mill Rythe Infant School on Hayling Island, Hampshire. Now Jenny was twenty-five years old, and it's at this point I was introduced to Jenny when visiting Jacqui Worthley, who was lodging with Ian and Juliet Ryall. Jenny was sitting in the corner of the lounge when I first saw her. She was drawing and painting pictures to illustrate Roger Price's first book, *In the Beginning*. I had seen her dancing in the meetings: Jenny loved praising the Lord with dancing.

I have told you already that I proposed to Jenny and we were married on the 8th of August 1981, which is 8/8/81. This date became very significant in our lives, as I have already mentioned but worth repeating. We were taught by Roger Price in one of his Bible studies that 8 means resurrection and that every letter in the New Testament Greek carries a numerical value. The name JESUS totals 888 which is resurrection, resurrection, resurrection. Very fitting because Jesus said, "I am the resurrection and the life and whosoever believes in me will not die but live forever." The date 8.8.81 meant to us that if we make Jesus No 1 we will have resurrection life in our marriage. We both endeavoured to make Jesus first in our lives and marriage. Jenny loved to reach out in prayer for a word from the Lord or a picture and move in the Holy Spirit. Her devotion to the Lord was steadfast, reading her Bible and praying daily, and she loved the Lord. Jenny was very witty and funny. When we had our three children Jenny was the one who read stories and prayed for them, tucking them up in bed. She let them be creative, building a den out of all the cushions on the sofas or making a mess painting.

Throughout the children's lives as they grew up,

Jenny kept the conversations going, sitting on their beds, talking to them through the difficult teenage years. Jenny stopped teaching after our first son was born, meaning that we lived off one wage during the first five years of their lives, because we believed the first five years of a child's life are the formative years. It was sometimes difficult to pay all the bills but we believed Jesus's words, "Seek ye first the Kingdom of God and all these things will be added unto you (meaning material possessions)." We both made sure we had at least one holiday a year in the summer. I can recall some of these times and places as follows:

Going on the Llangollen Canal in Wales, beautiful journey winding down the canal, stopping to go through the locks. The children loved winding the handle at the locks. Sometimes they had a go at the helm, causing a few scrapes and bangs. We used to stop off at a pub or café near the canal. Jenny, being a marvellous teacher, knew just what to do to make the children happy. When we moored up we would play a board game or have a meal and talk the day over.

We had some friends in the Dordogne in France that we went to see as a family, and spent a couple of weeks having a great holiday. We saw a lot of the sites around the Dordogne area. We loved it at night sitting down to a lovely meal and I loved the wine from the chateau owner's vineyard. I came back from that holiday so wound down and relaxed. Jenny was great at inspiring the children in art or writing.

Other places we went to over the years were Norfolk Broads, Isle of Wight, Cornwall, Lake District, New York, Canada, Houston, Texas, New Orleans, Lake Garda, Venice, Brittany, Florence, Rome, Center Parcs, Devon. We have some great videos and photographs of most of these holidays. We became and are a very close family enjoying traditional Christmas times together, playing board games and getting together at Easter time as a family. All these special times have built memories to look back on with joy and gratitude. I enjoyed making things for the children like a sand pit, blackboard easel, model fort, cars, a puppet theatre etc. Jenny was a hard worker keeping the house in tip-top condition. She was a cornerstone of traditional family life celebrating special times like Easter, Christmas. We had some very enjoyable times when Jenny cooked a lovely dinner and invited people to join us. We both loved our children so much and they brought us so much joy and happiness.

We started our married life in a mid-terraced house down Charles Avenue which was small but warm and cosy. Jenny then found a house in Croft Mead, which at the time was quiet, and looked over into a copse opposite the house. This was before Chichester became a university city, I believe nowadays it is full of students and a noisy place to live. We had many happy times in Croft Mead where we held our house group, and entertained many visitors having meals or BBQs. We then moved to live in a house called

Cherith, Fishbourne Road East, just on the edge of Chichester. It was a large, four-bedroomed house with two bathrooms, large lounge and dining room. We part owned the house with another couple in the fellowship. (They didn't live with us, though.) At first we felt a bit cut off from everyone as we didn't see any neighbours like we used to at Croft Mead. It was ideal for the children as the eldest two had just started Bishop Luffa School only a ten-minute walk away. One night we went to a pantomime in Southsea when we returned the house was under three feet of water. I carried the children one by one into the house, then Jenny.

We made a claim on our insurance and after a while we had a brand new Axminster carpet as well as other possessions replaced. After a few years living there we wanted to move to East Broyle Estate. After a long time on the marketplace we sold Cherith. We then moved in with our friends Ian and Juliet in their large house in Bosham for a while. We were very close to Ian and Juliet. We had some great Christmas times together along with their lovely daughter Michaela. We loved going to there for Sunday teas, too. Then we bought our present house on East Broyle Estate. It was great for our youngest, Jack, as he could just walk to Jessie Younghusband School in minutes. After a while we had an extension so that Peter could have his own room.

Wherever we lived Jenny had the gift of making it

a home, not just a place where we lived. She was very gifted in so many ways especially in art. Her drawings and paintings are still with us. I have described earlier how we continued attending Chichester Christian Fellowship and where we went after we left.

Earlier, I mentioned I would tell you what happened after we joined the new NFI Grace Church that was started in Chichester. It was all very exciting meeting new people, having great praise and worship along with good preaching by Steve Petch. After a few years, it moved into a warehouse in Chichester and was called The Grace Centre. We went out on the streets every now and again, giving out leaflets inviting people to Grace Church. One year we set up some marquees in front of the cathedral and cooked beefburgers and gave them out, engaging people with conversations about Jesus Christ and the good news of eternal life for those who believed. By this time, we had already moved to live in the house in North Chichester, a much-sought-after location only fifteen minutes' walk into the city centre, only five minutes' walk to the famous Festival Theatre. We both loved living in Chichester with its magnificent cathedral, South Downs National Park, Goodwood racing, beautiful harbour, lovely Wittering's beach, only two hours on the train to London to see a show in the West End.

After a while, Jenny felt she wanted to join the Chichester Baptist Church as she had quite a few friends there. I continued to go to Grace Church; sometimes I joined Jenny to go to an evening service at the Baptist church.

In 1997 Jenny had gone back to teaching at Easebourne Infant School near Midhurst. Teaching has become a very stressful profession with all the pressure from government departments. Jenny got excellent remarks from Ofsted inspections usually. In 2012 she was ill with a virus that was going round, and two of the teachers had two weeks off, but Jenny continued to soldier through. About a year or so later she began to get very tired and dizzy. Tests for labyrynthitis were done but the dizziness continued. Then the doctor thought it was her thyroid gland causing problems, so she went onto medication. This problem of dizziness went on for around five years. In December 2015, Jenny had a new doctor who looked at her notes and decided to give her all the blood tests under the sun. In January 2016, the doctor looking at the blood test results said there was something going on in her liver. She got an ultrasound scan organised for her at St Richard's Hospital.

A few weeks later, I was visiting my brother in Lincoln for a few days. I called in to see my friend Ken at a hospital in Leicester on my way home and I got a call from Jenny. "They want me to have a CT scan," she said. I assured her it wouldn't be serious and that they would just be trying to find out why she got dizzy. The next day, I was home and took Jenny into

St Richard's Hospital in Chichester for the scan. Two weeks later we had an appointment at the hospital to get the results. The news was bad. The consultant told us that there were tumours in Jenny's liver and gave it some long, fancy name. We both just couldn't believe what we were hearing, as Jenny didn't look that bad. We were told the next thing they wanted to do was a biopsy to see exactly what type of tumours they were.

Obviously, we asked people to pray for God to do a miracle and take the tumours out of her liver. The day came for the biopsy to be done, and, after taking Jenny to the hospital at 8am, I did some shopping and got home about 11am whereupon I just sat down and cried, calling on the Lord to heal Jenny. Little did I know she was still waiting to have the biopsy done, sitting on the trolley waiting to go in. She reached out to the Lord and He gave her a picture of a hosepipe that came to an end. Then she saw a hand put an extension fitting on the hosepipe and joined another section of hosepipe onto it. She took this to say that the Lord was going to extend her life and that she was not going to die.

A letter came through the post inviting Jenny to attend Queen Alexandra Hospital in Cosham to see an oncologist. The oncologist was a very nice man who explained very gently what they planned to do. A course of chemotherapy was the only option because the tumours were too big to take out. We started going to QA on a regular basis for Jenny to have the chemo. If you have never been to a hospital chemotherapy unit this is what it is like. There is a large room with about 40 comfortable padded chairs to sit on with a drip-feeder to one side. There are a number of nurses with their trolleys and laptops on them, plus a reception desk to one end. Everyone on the chairs is in different stages of treatment. Some people look fine but others look pale and very ill. We both found it a traumatic experience going there every week for several months with one in four breaks to give the body a rest. Jenny's lovely hair began to fall out and she was getting very weak and losing weight.

After six to eight months of chemotherapy, and seeing the consultants and having scans and blood tests done, Jenny felt she couldn't take any more. We had been in touch with a naturopathic practitioner who reckoned changing diet would help her and may even heal her. We also came across Ty Bollinger, an American Christian who had spent years researching cancer all over the world. There are testimonies on his website (The truth about cancer) of people being healed of cancer by changing their diet. I cannot cover all Ty says, as there are nine hours of YouTube videos to look at. Jenny started taking no sugar, as sugar makes tumours grow. Eating 20-30 apricot kernels a day, they have B7 chemical which attacks tumours. Ty discovered that a tribe who eat apricot kernels in a daily diet never had cancer. I bought a juicer to juice such organic vegetables as carrots, as a substance in carrots kills tumours. We did many such things that would take a book to explain everything to you. There are already a whole load of books in the marketplace explaining how to combat cancer through diet. In these books there are testimonies of people getting healed by following a strict diet. Also there is information about cannabis oil for healing cancer.

We did hear about a private clinic called Dove Clinic in Twyford, Hampshire. We went to see Dr Kenyon and went through with a course of vitamin C treatment. Also another treatment which I cannot recall but, again, you can find all that they offer on the Dove Clinic website. We spent about £12,000 with Dove Clinic, battling away against this awful disease. We even considered flying to a clinic in Bangkok but we couldn't get travel insurance, so thought it too risky and expensive, as it was going to cost £60,000. If anything went wrong the daily cost of a hospital was going to be at least a thousand pounds. We were willing to go but in the end we felt the Lord gave us wisdom to not do so.

On the spiritual side we went for everything that was available to us in the Word of God. We came across a lady's testimony who was called Dodie Osteen from Houston, Texas. Dodie was the wife of John Osteen who was the leader of a large church out there. The Lord healed Dodie of liver cancer some years ago now. The consultants said there was nothing they could do. You can read her little book or see her testimony on YouTube. We loved watching John Osteen preach on faith for a miracle. We read lots of books on healing from the Lord. We contacted lots of Christian organisations to ask for prayer for healing for Jenny. Daily we called out to God for a miracle and confessed about 40 promises on healing a day. The Bible tells us that death and life are in the power of the tongue. People have been healed by God by just confessing His word and standing in faith on His Word. We went to healing meetings and had Jenny prayed for and laying on of hands. Jesus said, "You shall lay hands on the sick and they shall be healed." At some of these meetings the Lord touched Jenny in a mighty way. Many people were healed in these meetings of all sorts of diseases and physical problems too many to recall and tell you about here.

Time was ticking on. One day the nurses and Dr Kenyon said that the tumours were growing and they couldn't help Jenny anymore.

Earlier in the summer my phone rang and it was showing Ishmael's number. I answered it, but no one answered back. I had bought some books from Ishmael a few years previously direct so I had his number on my phone, but never phoned him. Ishmael is a famous Christian songwriter minister. I sent a text back to him saying I was sorry to have missed his call. Apparently he had been on the golf course, and his phone was in his bag. His phone had mysteriously rung my number by itself. I think it was God who made his phone ring mine. Anyway, he answered my text and I explained what was going on with Jenny. At ten o'clock the next day he was standing at the door saying, "Hello, I'm Ish." He had had leukaemia and cancer, and went through a very tough time having chemotherapy and got better, so he had lots of empathy for anyone suffering with cancer. Ish was a tremendous encouragement and blessing to us as we travelled along the way. God bless Ishmael.

We had ladies from the Chichester Baptist Church visit us on a weekly basis to pray for and with Jenny. There was a team of ladies who cooked and brought meals around for us when Jenny was having chemo and later when I was caring for Jenny and running round trying to get the proper drugs. It was a superb group of ladies from the Baptist church. I also had visits from Ellen Wilde and Ken Benjamin who are leaders at the Baptist church which was a great help. God bless Ellen and Ken. Also I had support and help from the guys at Grace Church. I felt the power of prayer coming from Heaven.

It was now summer 2017. Jenny was feeling a lot of pain and was advised by the doctor and friends to contact St Wilfrid's Hospice in Chichester and ask for a visit from their nurse. We had a visit from a very nice lady who took lots of notes and examined Jenny. At this point, Jenny felt just uncomfortable with some pain. A cocktail of pain-killing drugs was prescribed for me to collect and make sure that the right drugs were given at the right time. I made a spreadsheet to make sure I did everything correctly. Jenny did go into the hospice for a couple of weeks for observation so as to be prescribed the right drugs for her. Afterwards we were given a medical bed with a special mattress to stop bedsores, plus a commode and a walker. We put the bed in our downstairs bedroom which looked out across the school fields towards Chichester Cathedral. From the bed, when it was raised, Jenny could see the cathedral. Only a few years ago she had painted some wonderful watercolour paintings of the cathedral.

As time went on, my lovely Jenny was getting thinner and weaker. It was now the beginning of September 2017. Could she make her 62nd birthday on the 21st of September? It was a very traumatic, very humiliating and devastating time seeing Jenny in so much pain. I often used to have to call a special number in the middle of the night for a nurse to come out to Jenny to administer pain relief. The nurses came every day to clean and make Jenny as comfortable as possible. God bless the nurses. On the 9th of September we had a visit from the consultant from St Wilfrid's Hospice who told us Jenny had only got days to go before she would die.

At that time my friends from Ashford, Bob and Jacqui Lambert, were around in Bognor Regis visiting

Bob's mother. Jacqui moved in that week and slept in the cabin in our garden. She was a great comfort to me because she was a fully trained nurse as well as a friend. She was able to comfort Jenny by knowing what to say and do, also to comfort me as things progressed. On the 17th of September about 5.30pm, I went into see Jenny and to change the CD that was playing worship music. It was on the eighth track of a Don Moen CD and it was the eighth day from when the consultant doctor from St Wilfrid's has told us Jenny was going to die. Jenny's laboured breathing suddenly went quieter, and quieter, and eventually stopped. I was shocked and didn't know what to do, so I ran to get Jacqui and Bob who were in the cabin. Jacqui felt for a pulse and said she had gone. I wept. Jacqui was there at the beginning of our relationship and she was there at the end. Thank you, Lord, for precious friends like Bob and Jacqui. I love them so much.

The Bible says about our body dying in 1 Corinthians 15:42-44 that we are sown in dishonour, raised in glory, sown in weakness, raised in power. It's a fact that those who believe in Jesus Christ will have their bodies raised, just like Jesus's body was raised from the dead. In the meantime Jenny is in Heaven, I am certain, having a wonderful time. It's really sad for those of us who are left behind, as we all miss her so much. I have to keep reminding myself one day I will see her again. I never knew what grieving was until Jenny died.

We had a celebration of Jenny's life at the Chichester Baptist Church which was packed out and was a very emotional time for everyone there. The week before I had attended my sister Janet's funeral in Boston, Lincolnshire. Janet was 80 years old; she died of lung cancer. I miss Janet, too. When Janet and I talked about Jesus her eyes lit up and she told me she prayed to Jesus every night. I am certain there are many secret believers who never go to church, but pray to God and have some sort of a relationship going on that nobody but them knows about. I am guessing we will get quite a surprise when we get to Heaven at all the people we had never dreamed we would see standing there. People on their very last breath call out to God to save them, I am sure he listens to every silent prayer that's thought. I am sure I will see my sister Janet in Heaven one day.

All the usual questions came running round my mind. Why didn't God heal Jenny?

Why did God allow Jenny to get cancer? The answer is we don't know. Ros Price sent me a CD with Roger's talk on the Sovereignty of God. This has been the only thing that makes any sense to me at the moment. I feel so sad for my three children who miss their mum so much. The comfort is that we will all be together one day, in our resurrection bodies forever with the Lord in a new Heaven and new earth. I am writing this in Spain on the 22nd of March; it is eighteen months after Jenny died. There are days when something triggers me off grieving for the death of Jenny. It happens in the most unusual times and places. Christmas, Easter, Mother's Day, her birthday, our wedding anniversary: they all trigger an emotion.

Thank you, Lord, for giving me 36 years with Jenny Davis: one day I will see you again. I imagine Jenny in Heaven in front of a large canvas or wall, splashing paint, making wonderful pictures with colours of the world's spectrum.

In the November after Jenny had died in the September I visited my son in Amsterdam to see him, but also to see the places Jenny had told me about when she had visited some two or three years previously. I went to the museums and art galleries and usual sites to be visited when in Amsterdam. On the Sunday I went to a church called Liberty Church near van Gogh's museum. Right at the end of the meeting the leader's wife stood up and said she had a word from the Lord for someone. The word was that you think what has happened, has happened and that now you just have to put up with it and get on with life, coping the best you can. But the Lord loves you so much, He wants to heal and restore you. The lady didn't know that those were my very thoughts in the morning about what's happened has happened, I just have to get on and cope. Since then, I have hung onto that word from the Lord. Gradually He is restoring my soul as in Psalm 23.

It is now the middle of May back home in England, I am sitting in the cabin writing, wondering what God has in store for the next years of my life on planet earth. Whatever the Lord has planned I know for certain this life is but a vapour in the light of eternity. We used to sing a song that says eyes have not seen ears have not heard that which God has prepared for those that love Him. Jesus said just before His departure from planet earth, I go to prepare a place for you, in my father's house are many mansions. Kind of strange to us to say in my father's house are many mansions, but I am guessing it's a whole new vast, large dimension in Heaven that we cannot possibly comprehend with our present natural mind, even if we try to explain it.

I hope you have enjoyed reading *Ello Duck*, the journey of Mike Davis. I hope you have picked up one or two things that have helped you along your journey in life. We are all very different individuals with all our different ways of looking at life on planet earth. One thing is for sure: whoever you are and wherever you come from, the Lord Jesus Christ loves you and would like you to know Him. His love is deeper than the deepest sea, wider than the widest ocean, higher than the highest mountain. May God bless you on your journey through this life.

Lightning Source UK Ltd.
Milton Keynes UK
UKHW010309180719
346343UK00001B/13/P